REBELLIOUS
Aging

A Self-Help Guide for the Old Hippie at Heart

MARGARET NASH

ISBN: 978-1-5118571-5-4

Contents

Introduction

"Time, Time, Time, See What's Become of Me..."

"Don't let the corporations, newspapers, or statistics hold a picture before you of old age, declining years, decrepitude, senility, and uselessness. Reject it, for it is a lie. Refuse to be hypnotized by such propaganda. Affirm life—not death. Get a vision of yourself as happy, radiant, successful, serene, and powerful."

Joseph Murphy—*The Power of Your Subconscious Mind*

This is a book about transitions; the transitions of life that sometimes hit you hard—like retirement, kids leaving home, divorce, relocation—or waking up one morning and realizing you are no longer a spring chicken.

It is aimed primarily at the *Old Hippie at Heart*, but is for anybody who feels the need to defy the rules and norms society tries to force on us—media driven and mostly to do with selling something.

1

The *Old Hippie at Heart* is the name I have given those of us who came of age in the 1960s, enthusiastically embraced the whole counter culture movement, and then went on to live relatively normal lives. We are in disguise. And despite normal appearances, we retain a fierce independence, a healthy distrust of authority, and have always been rebels at heart. No matter how conventional we appear on the surface, and no matter how often we play the society game, an *Old Hippie, a Free Spirit,* still lives deep within the recesses of the heart and wants to come out and play.

If you are an *Old Hippie at Heart,* the label will resonate with you like an old friend or long-lost soul mate. You won't have to stop and figure out if it fits you—it either does or it doesn't.

You are most likely a Baby Boomer, born between 1946 and 1964; but it's not about age, it's about *attitude,* and you have plenty of that.

You may have been a teenager or college student during the 60s.

You definitely were a Beatles fanatic. Then you discovered the Stones…

You remember where you were and what you were doing during the weekend of Woodstock and why you missed it. You pretend you really regret not being there, in spite of the rain, mud, and lack of sanitation.

You wholeheartedly embraced the counter culture and everything about it; you wore beads and no makeup, jeans and tie-dye tee shirts, and your hair was long and unkempt. You adored Bob Dylan and Crosby Stills & Nash, and you desperately wanted to be identified as a true believer. We won't mention sex and drugs…

Your parents never fully recovered.

And then you graduated from college and life happened. You had to get on with earning a living, raising a family and being *normal.* But there has always been something that is a little *weird* about you—according to your family—and they still hope you are going through a phase you will outgrow.

You won't.

Chances are these days you no longer live in a commune, smoke dope (well, maybe some of you), or follow a macrobiotic diet. You gave up Transcendental Meditation about two months after signing up, and makeup is your best friend now. Jeans are passé, and you love your hairdresser. You don't look like a hippie on the outside.

At Heart an Old Hippie

But *at heart* you still yearn for the non-conformist life, and something you can't explain calls you. Let's distinguish here between the *Old Hippie* and the *Old Hippie at Heart.* The genuine *Old Hippie* is a rare sighting, depending on where you live. Here in the mountains of Mexico you see them roll into town in an old Jeep or camper, ponytailed and crusty; they load up on supplies and then head quickly back out to the country. They are artists, writers, organic farmers. Yellow-stained fingers from years of smoking roll-ups. These are serious people and have very strong opinions about life.

The *Old Hippie at Heart*, on the other hand, is in camouflage. On the surface we appear reasonably conventional but at heart still *Rebels* and *Free Spirits*, and sometimes the disguise drops a bit. A giveaway may be a liking for ethnic jewelry, or maybe a mid-life throwing away of a good selling job to become a Reiki therapist. We've been doing yoga for years (although this is now mainstream so not very rebellious) and feel cool driving an old car. But we like having money, just not ostentatiously.

If you are an *Old Hippie at Heart*, then like Buck the dog in the *Call of the Wild*, as you are getting older this yearning to give rein to your non-conformist spirit may be getting more insistent. It shows in your new vegan diet, or your recently started organic garden, or your newly revived political activism for gays, women, animals, human rights, and the environment. You have switched your money making career for something in alternative healing or art.

You may be into de-cluttering and want to move back to the land. As long as you don't have to give up your car.

You don't know why, but you have a craving for a simpler life.

Aging!

More importantly, you may be looking for alternative ways to age that are different from the mainstream, that are fun and relevant. Me too. I want to age with my unconventional, cantankerous disposition still fighting battles against accepted norms that I don't like, and making myself heard. I don't intend to fade into the woodwork, and I refuse to *"go gentle into that good night."*

Neither do I want to retire to the golf course or take up knitting. The word 'hobby' appalls me for some reason. It sounds like something inane you do to just fill your time, keep you distracted, and out of trouble until you die. *"But it keeps your mind active!"* I hear you say. Yes ,well, maybe.

I'm not interested in dressing 'age appropriately'. I like to wear my hair long. I prefer dressing down to dressing up. I have a horror of being drugged up with prescription medication just because I am getting older, and I don't buy into the paradigm that old age is a disease. And despite what 'they' want us to believe, I believe we can be vibrant, healthy, and fearless as we age, but it's crucial to avoid 'their' interference.

So *Rebellious Aging* is about balking against and ignoring the messages some parts of society are cramming down our throats about growing older. The media and corporations for the most part seem to want us to be scared. Why? Simple. Follow the money.

We aging Boomers are big business. *They* are hoping we will spend money trying to assuage the fear they are trying to instill in us. *They* want us to spend more and more money on prescription drugs, on yet more insurance, on pensions, on health care plans. *They* believe old age is an illness and we must take a plethora of drugs to ameliorate the *inevitable* disabilities we will suffer from. And *they* will try to scare us into retirement villages even if we don't want to go, by insinuating that we will be unable to look after ourselves and will be a burden to family and friends. If we don't buckle down we will be lonely, too.

Aargh! No wonder we dread growing older—we are being scared to death!

It doesn't have to be like that! We Boomers, Woodstock Generationers, and *Old Hippies* still rule the world! We have since the 60s and will continue right up until the very end. You and I have clout. You and I can think for ourselves. You and I have dominated every era we have lived in, changed paradigms, and been trail blazers.

We can be trail blazers for growing older. We've done it before. We can do it again.

The opposite of courage isn't cowardice, it's conformity.

Fearless Aging

Rebellious Aging is a book about handling transitions, growing older, *and enjoying it!* This is the time of your life when you can do what you want. You no longer have to care what people think of you, you don't have to spend time with people you don't want to spend time with and you can say what you think. It's time to have fun and do the things that *Old Hippie* has been longing to do.

This book is designed to help you find your purpose in life right now, and pursue the *ultimate human adventure* with courage and a pioneering spirit. It's about discovering new ways to move on to the next stage of life with the same spirit that you had in the 60s.

Transitions

Maybe you are facing some major changes in your life right now and as a result feel a little lost. Your kids are leaving home; you are going through a divorce (maybe your second or third), finding a new partner, relocating to somewhere exotic (read cheaper), facing retirement and having a good hard and uncomfortable look at your finances. Your health may be challenging you, your parents are getting really old, and you're just darn scared sometimes of what growing older holds in store for you. The mirror is no longer your friend.

And if you are an *Old Hippie* and have lived a little rebelliously, you may be finding these transitions especially tough right now. The boomer generation is putting itself through lots of major transitions all at once, at an unprecedented rate, compared to the generations before us.

We mostly don't live in our hometowns—we moved away long ago—or go to church anymore, or have the usual stable structures to support us during transitions. We rebelled against those structures and institutions, right?

This book is for you if you want to get through these transitions with your sanity intact; especially the transition of growing older. You are simply not prepared to 'fade into the sunset' but prefer to age *your* way and have fun while doing it.

It is not about aging gracefully or dressing appropriately or whether you should have plastic surgery, or what is the best health care plan? Those subjects, important as it is to make prudent plans, are not the purview of this book. It will not cover health, finances, or retirement plans. Or death and wills. I repeat, it is important to make prudent plans for yourself and look after business. But not here.

It is an *alternative* coaching guide to aging. It's designed to help you revive that *Old Hippie* spirit and push back against the pressures society puts us under as we grow older.

A rallying cry to push back; think for yourself; age rebelliously!

Hippiedom! Do You Remember it?

For a brief period in the late 1960s and early 1970s hippies dominated the Western cultural landscape and drove their parents and families crazy with worry. Hippies attempted to challenge all the accepted norms of the day; and although they constituted only a small section of society, made a huge impression on the world.

We *Old Hippies* are sometimes referred to as the *Woodstock Generation*, a niche within the Baby Boomers, and we tend to make up the rules as we go along. If you are a little older than the generation I'm talking about, perhaps you relate more to being a Bohemian or a Beatnik. That's fine—come on in—you're one of us.

We are legendary for forging our own paths in life, especially in the spheres of work, relationships, health, and spirituality. And we have created new paradigms for living at every stage along the way. We are pioneers. We think of ourselves as heroic in many ways.

Here are a few areas where we have left our mark on the world: alternative medicine, working mothers, men sharing child rearing, an exodus from organized religion, new methods of practicing spirituality (mostly from the Far East), blended families with friendly exes, same-sex marriage, women's rights, gay rights, environmental protection, yoga and meditation, and new work patterns. Oh and of course we take credit for stopping a war!

7

Many (and I plead the fifth) at least 'experimented' with mind-altering drugs, especially marijuana. Some even inhaled. It was all in the interest of 'expanding our consciousness', of course. You name it and we tried it, started it, or changed it. It didn't always work as well as expected but we did it our way and that's what seemed to count.

And yes, there were some notable casualties along the way. There was definitely a dark side to these turbulent times. We watched in horror and dismay as some of our most iconic musicians were lost to drug overdoses. Divorce rates escalated. We became intolerant in the name of tolerance and there was a self righteous air to a lot of our protests. There is no denying that.

But still, it was an interesting, exciting, and eye-opening time in which to grow up. And now we former hippies are getting older and many of us are having our very own aging crisis. How *do* alternative thinkers grow older? We always thought we defined cool, so how do we make growing old, cool? There has to be a way!

Alternative Life-Coaching

This book will provide you with a step-by-step process for handling transitions—for surviving and thriving—in a way that guarantees you will feel empowered to *carry on.* It provides you with clear techniques and procedures to guide you at each stage of your journey.

The questions are designed to help you discover your 'true self' and retrieve those fragments of your soul that you may have lost somewhere along the way. It will help you reconnect to your roots.

The processes, techniques, and metaphors are alternative; they aren't mainstream and you won't get them from your doctor or in the psychiatrist's office. You can safely try them at home with no training and at no cost and with no side effects. I think you will like them.

This is a mixture, a confluence, of my hippie roots (with those alternative influences), my business background (with its emphasis on what works and gets results), and my personal life experiences.

At the end of this book you will have a clearer idea of who you are, how you want to age, and what your purpose is in life, for right now.

Please read on…

Chapter 1

"To be on Your Own, With no Direction Home, a Complete Unknown...": Crisis Time!

I grew up in the Deep South, the daughter of a Presbyterian preacher. Like many Baby Boomers, I was a teenager when the Beatles hit the world stage—like a nuclear explosion—and I was instantly a convert to whatever they had to offer. I embraced the whole shebang and totally identified with the revolutionary nature of the times. I loved the music, the clothes, the ideas. It was all so daring and exciting. I know all the words to Sgt. Pepper and to every Bob Dylan song. Coming from a conservative background as a preacher's kid in the Deep South, this was no small deal. You had to be *brave* to join the hippie club back then.

Like many of us, I desperately wanted to be cool and accepted as part of the counter-culture; I *tuned in, turned on, and dropped out*. Well sort of. In my heart anyway. I still had Daddy's credit card tucked in my back pocket. I stopped wearing make-up and let my hair grow long and wild. I went barefoot.

Ok, it sounds kind of tame. But it was impossible to be part of that movement and maintain traditional attitudes towards life. A lot of us were marked forever, in good ways and bad. But most of us would not trade being part of that era for anything.

Selling Out

I visited England the summer after college graduation, met and married an Englishman, and started raising a family. And like many of my ilk, pushed against traditional norms while still trying to be an accepted part of society. Being a rebel can sometimes be tiring and being poor is a drag. After awhile I just wanted to fit in and make some money. *"I was tired of being poor..."*

I sort of hung around the fringes. And I eventually sold out and got into the business world where I was highly successful for several decades.

But the *Old Hippie* never truly left me. It kept calling, nagging at me, and showing itself in different ways when I least expected it. In my 40s I was about as far away from my roots as you can get, working as a sales trainer for international tech companies in Europe. I was almost embarrassingly good at it, competitive and aggressive. I never knew I had that side to me—it kind of intrigued and horrified me in equal parts.

But eventually I started weaning myself from my business career (and all the money), as I became interested in alternative psychology and complementary methods of healing. I embraced Neuro-linguistic Programming (NLP), hypnosis and the whole personal development movement. I went to London for an introductory weekend course in NLP and emerged 4 years later in a sort of trance—once again, changed forever.

I liked that it challenged orthodox medicine and psychology. It was daring and new. I became caught between two worlds, business and alternative, and not totally fitting in either of them. One of them made money; one didn't. Go ahead and guess.

Then my kids grew up and I moved from England back to the States, and eventually to Mexico. This was precipitated by several factors: a friendly divorce, the kids leaving home, and a personal financial crisis resulting from the events of Sept 11, 2001.

So it was that I woke up one day, after an odyssey from England to Houston to Mexico, with a new husband (Mexican this time), a new home, and in a new country—and I knew I had somehow lost the plot.

All those transitions, all coming at once, had left me spiritually exhausted and feeling like I didn't know who I was anymore. I was emotionally bankrupt. Have you been there? You feel totally on your own.

Where Was My Rebel?

I had been sure of my identity while living in England—an American living and working in a foreign country—but I had lost my *roles* when I moved back to the other side of the Atlantic. In England I had been a wife, a mother, and a professional, with a clear idea of who I was and where I fit in.

Now there was a big blank, where before there had been an interesting life. For the first time ever, I had nothing to talk about when I met new people. I became dull and confused about who I was. It was my first inkling of how deeply we identify with the roles we play in life and how devastating it can be when those roles disappear.

In my new life in Mexico, at least I didn't have to work any more to survive and I had no more financial issues. So I filled my time with Spanish lessons, art classes, Pilates, and lunch dates with friends. I threw myself wholeheartedly into enjoying my retirement. Trying to, at any rate.

But I wasn't happy. Something *big* was missing and I didn't know where to look for it. I felt stuck, with low energy and a bad Internet habit. I also felt like a spoilt brat for not being content with my comfortable life. My attempt to find a new identity and new roles with the activities listed above just simply wasn't working. And somehow the idea of having *activities* (hobbies!) to fill my time, well, it just felt like I was on my way out of the game and coasting downhill. I was disconnected from the mainstream, no longer a player, just on the sideline. *"Like a rolling stone..."*

Where was the old *Rebel, the Pioneer, the brave Warrior, the Free Spirit,* who had moved abroad after college and made a life for herself in foreign lands? Where was the *Old Hippie?* I felt alienated and I seemed to have forgotten how to live my life.

What in the world do you do with yourself when you no longer have to work for a living? I had always faced life head on and confronted problems with fierce determination. I had been a working mother bringing up three lively children. I had overcome the difficulties of living in a foreign country without the usual support systems around me and I had created a successful business career against the odds.

It had been stressful, and it had also been exciting. Most importantly, it had been *my* life with *my* choices and consequences. I had at least felt authentic and I was proud of myself.

Now I was forced to search for a new sense of purpose, of identity —my sense of place.

Transitions

One thing was for sure; I was in transition and didn't realize it. As well as all the other changes I was going through, I was getting older and time felt like it was running out on me. An underlying sense of unease, of anxiety set in. Where did I go from here?

I was left facing some very uncomfortable questions that I now know are typical of transition periods: Is this what my life had come to? Had all the challenges, the experiences and lessons of life, the painful self-growth—had it evolved to this? To become a 'lady who lunches' and then hurries off to art class?

These questions were disconcerting and I was deeply dissatisfied.

This deep dissatisfaction was in fact my salvation, because it propelled me on a journey to retrieve my soul and reconnect with my former passion for life. It also forced me to discover who I *really* was without any roles to define me.

This was my *Hero's Journey*, which ultimately led me to finding my gifts and treasures and re-designing my life.

What's So Special About Us?

Is there anything different or special about the crises we *Old Hippies* and Baby Boomers are experiencing from the generations before us? If so, what is it?

Lots! In the 'good old days', when aging crisis time rolled around and people were faced with these heavy life questions— *What is the purpose of my life? Is this all there is? Is it too late to live my dream?* —these classic questions were usually dealt with in the context of a traditional, supportive community.

Everybody confronts these questions at some point—maybe in the 40s during the archetypal midlife crisis, or in the 60s with the challenges of retirement. However, back in the 'good old days' they were faced in the comfort zone of family, religious institutions and familiar surroundings.

So most people were able to cope with the crisis and get through it with their sanity intact, without resorting to prescription drugs or alcohol.

And then we *Hippies* came along and changed everything.

It's Probably Our Own Fault

Today things are *very* different. As we rebelled against all things traditional, some good things got lost along the way, such as stable family life and supportive religious and social communities. We chose to live unconventionally and there is always a price to pay for turning against the accepted standards of the day.

In unprecedented ways, as we now approach our 60s and 70s, we are piling on extra stresses during these vulnerable times in our lives: divorce, remarriage, career changes, and relocation. This is happening much, much more often than it did to our predecessors.

We human beings aren't designed to handle too much change at one time. If we do we risk throwing ourselves into confusion and depression or other forms of stress related illness. Too many changes all at once—never a good idea. They trigger the fight or flight response and our bodies just can't cope.

I know this from experience because I live thousands of miles away from my grown-up children in England. I'm remarried. I live in yet another foreign country, Mexico. I went through all my transitions at once and I know how overwhelming and disconcerting it can be. And because I've always wanted to do things my way, and live life my way, I didn't have the usual supports or role models on hand to help me through.

But I somehow survived, and eventually thrived, and based on what I have learned, I *don't* believe going through transitions has to be as painful, or quite as scary, as some of us experience it. Challenging and exciting, yes: painful and scary, not always.

And I *do* believe that we need to create new paradigms for aging that take our *Old Hippie* roots, as well as our crazy modern lives, into account. Plus relationships held together by Skype, email, and Facebook.

At 65 we may have another third of our lives to live and *we want to spend that time in an interesting way*, not filling it with hobbies.

Follow me on my journey to find my way out of the dark forest I found myself in. It may help you in yours.

The Hero's Journey

The book roughly follows the outline of the *Hero's Journey*, which is a metaphor for the search for your 'true heart's desire' and for connecting with your life purpose. It is an allegory for the eternal quest for special knowledge and for uncovering hidden secrets about the meaning of life. A subterranean journey into the caverns of the subconscious mind.

Throughout history legends have been told of the *Hero's Journey* to find a lost treasure: King Arthur and the search for the Holy Grail, the search for El Dorado, the city of gold, the quest for the Fountain of Youth, or the Philosopher's Stone. Homer's Odyssey and Pilgrim's Progress are examples of *Hero's Journeys*.

In many ways the whole hippie thing can be seen as a *Hero's Journey* into new horizons. So you know how to do this.

> *"The basic story of the hero journey involves giving up where you are, going into the realm of adventure, coming to some kind of symbolically rendered realization, and then returning to the field of normal life."*

> Joseph Henderson—*Ancient Myths and Modern Man*

The journey this book will take you on includes:

Fighting dragons, which are metaphors for anything that stops you from finding your purpose. In particular, the dragons of *fear* and *despair*, and the limiting messages society has instilled in you about how you should live your life in your later years.

On the journey you will be challenged to slay the dragon of fear of aging by facing it rebelliously.

Meeting your archetypes; those defining aspects of your personality that have been part of you your whole life. Becoming aware of archetypes will help you finally fill in the missing pieces that can explain who you really are and what you could best be doing with your life. You will discover your "authentic self". The Old Hippie is a take on the Rebel and Pioneer archetypes.

Rewriting your story to fit this new stage of your life. This *Guide* will show you how to identify the outdated scripts you want to rebel against and mold them into new, more empowering ones to live by.

Searching for gifts and treasure, a quest which will uncover your unique gifts, talents and current purpose in life.

Discovering your 'true heart's desire' and learning how to adapt it in a practical way to your current circumstances in life, while honoring your past in all its glory.

Returning home from the Hero's Journey and manifesting your new purpose.

When you have taken this journey I hope you will feel courageous and *fierce* about growing older, and that you will have found your sense of place, your unique niche in life.

You will learn how to survive and thrive transitions.

I hope you will be feeling defiant once again and up for the challenge of fighting against the way society expects you to age.

For this reason I encourage you to answer the questions and do the exercises in the book. These are the steps I went through on my *Hero's Journey* to rewrite my script and learn how to face my future fearlessly. I know they are effective. However, you have to *actually* do them if you want them to work for you...

The Consequences of Not Heeding the Call

Transition times, episodes of uncertainty and change, can be the most valuable times of our lives. They can be painful, and yet we become alive and open to new ideas and to personal growth. If you are in transition I urge you to view this time of your life as an adventure and an opportunity to evolve and develop like never before. The best is yet to come! Please heed the call!

Of course, at every step along the way, you have the choice to heed the call or not. You have the choice whether or not to begin your *Hero's Journey*, face your fears head on and take action, or do nothing and remain safe in your comfort zone.

Sometimes we need to hit rock bottom before we can start climbing upwards.

Experiencing the 'dark night of the soul' is the quintessential starting place for the *Hero's Journey*. So recognize where you are and take advantage of this unique and wonderful opportunity.

Starting the journey can be scary. You are heading into unknown territory. But if you ignore the call you could remain perpetually *lost in transition*, unwilling to move forward and unable to go back. *Stuck! Afraid of aging! Dying of boredom!*

This book will help you rewrite your life story into one that works for you and reflects where you are right now and what you need right now. It will take you through the exact processes I went through that proved so effective for me in creating a radically new life, that I enjoy…now.

My journey took 10 years. Yours can be *much* shorter if you follow the steps in this book. You can accelerate your time in transition. What you have here is a combination of my expertise as a life coach, hypnotherapist and personal development trainer, my life experiences, my business approach with its emphasis on results, my background of growing up in the 60s and being a rebel, and a practical guide to getting it all to work.

Are you ready? I'm excited to be taking this hero's journey with you. So hop in your hippie van and let's go…

Chapter 2

"Ch-ch-ch-ch-Changes...": Transition Shock

"You can take your instructions and your guidance from others, but you must find your own path just like one of Arthur's knights seeking the grail in the forest."

Joseph Campbell—*Pathways to Bliss*

Transitions come in two kinds: one is the sudden, unexpected crisis, such as death of someone close to you, an accident, ill health, the breakup of a relationship; the second is the gradual kind that you thought you were prepared for, such as kids leaving home, retirement, relocation, and...aging.

If you are in the either kind of transition—the sudden crisis or the gradual change—then you may be suffering transition shock. Shock usually comes with the first kind, the unexpected change. This is the worst possible time to be making decisions about your life, your finances, where you are going to live, and who with. Stop! It's time to cocoon and just give yourself some breathing space. You can't force a cocoon—it simply has to take the time it needs to transform into a butterfly.

Shock is nature's way of dealing with overwhelm; if you cannot cope with what is going on, your body and mind go into denial. *I'll think about that tomorrow.*

We all know the sage advice to postpone moving or making any big decisions after the death of a spouse or partner. And we all know about people who don't follow that advice and who marry on the rebound, or spend all their inherited money, or sell their home and move to Spain. And usually regret it.

If you are in the second kind of transition, the gradual kind, then you may be feeling stuck, or frozen like a deer in headlights. Something is wrong but you're not sure what. You thought you had prepared yourself for the change, but you don't seems to be coping so well. Growing older is a prime example of this sort of change.

Growing older kind of sneaks up on you; one day you look in the mirror and go into a kind of mini-shock of non-recognition, a sort of weird depression where you don't know how you should be interacting with people anymore.

If you are in either sort of crisis it may feel as if you are lost in a deep forest and can't find your way out. There are no guideposts and your compass is broken. You may feel you have hit rock bottom emotionally and don't know where to turn.

If this is your situation I suggest you simply stop! Stop fighting it, stop thinking about it, stop trying to fix it. It's time to cocoon, reorient and give yourself some breathing space. Cocooning involves deliberately doing nothing, making no decisions and setting no goals. Vegetate, join Netflix and watch films, read, do nothing. It's surprisingly relaxing.

I travel quite a lot and every time I return home, I go into a mini-transition shock. I know that for the first 3 or 4 days after I'm back, I don't like anything, I don't want to do anything, and I don't want to see anybody. I dislike my life intensely but don't know what I want instead. I miss wherever I was while traveling.

So I have learned to just cocoon and do nothing. I indulge myself in being totally lazy, and sure enough, in about 3 days I'm back to normal. It's something you cannot rush, just like you cannot force a butterfly out of its cocoon too early.

And the interesting thing is that in this cocooning period lots of things about your life become crystal clear and your perspective is sharpened.

When you are lost in the woods a professional tracker would tell you the best thing to do is to stop. You are most likely panicking, and wandering around in circles. This is the dangerous time you're most likely to fall in a ditch. You've got to find your own path if you want to get your life back. But you won't find it by panicking.

In my case, I felt energized and in control while moving countries, from England to the US, and then to Mexico, getting remarried, and sorting out a new place to live. I had to be; it was all about survival, making it work. I at least knew what my role was and I had clear goals of finding a place to live and getting resettled. Change on its own doesn't necessarily put you in shock.

It was afterwards, when the crisis was over and I was settled in with some semblance of stability in my life that the reaction set in. I began to feel numb. This didn't make sense and took me by surprise. I had already made it through the bad times, or so I thought. I should be happy—or at least contented. What was going on? Why did I feel so stuck, so lacking in enthusiasm?

What was going on was that my old life story was out of date and needed revising. My compass was broken. Because of all the transitions I needed new roles to step into, new strategies for how to live my life.

I wanted to find out who I was now in relation to who I used to be. And although I couldn't go back to the past, I knew there was something there that I wanted to relate to again. I was an *Old Hippie at Heart*, so where had all that rebellious energy gone?

It was necessary for me to recognize this before I could move on. I was in between lives, in between stories. I needed to cocoon and reorient.

A Great Place to Be!

Being lost in the forest is a great place to be!

Why do I say this? I say this because while you may not have deliberately chosen to be there, getting lost in the forest of confusion is the beginning of wisdom, the first step to retrieving your soul and finding your passion.

The journey always starts with a crisis of some sort, the transition, which in turn triggers a deep soul sickness that forces the hero (you and me) to search for a solution. Soul sickness is what can cause feelings of despair and panic. These feelings in turn cause you to feel lost, stuck, and willing to do anything to find your way out.

That's why it's important to stop, relax, take a deep breath and acknowledge where you are, and how you got here. Breathe, relax; it's going to be OK. There is a way out of here and you're going to end up feeling better than when you started.

Jonathan—in Transition

Jonathan had just retired and moved from the States to Mexico, to start a new life. He had had a long and successful career in business and was more than ready to get out. He wanted a complete change, something adventurous and exciting.

He expected to jump into his new life straight away and began to get impatient with delays in finding the right house to live in, and getting settled. He wanted to get on with his life! He didn't want to deal with *stuff*.

As the weeks went by, he and his wife had to move several times because of problems with accommodation. He began to lose his enthusiasm for his new environment. Nothing felt settled and he started feeling depressed and began missing his old life. He stopped going out and would follow his wife around the house when she was at home. He became indecisive and unable to accomplish even the smallest tasks.

He longed for his old life where it was familiar and he knew how things worked. He wanted to get back to his comfort zone, forgetting that that was exactly what he had worked hard to get away from, because it had grown boring and unfulfilling.

His wife, however, found it easy to make new friends and find things to do. He became a nuisance to her, relying on her for everything, and she wondered what had happened to her once "alpha male" husband. Their relationship was under threat.

Jonathan was in transition shock. He was wandering in the forest, lost. He didn't know who he was any more and he had no guideposts to help him live his life. He was in retirement crisis and it was compounded by his move to another country. What he needed was time and guidance and someone to assure him that his feelings were normal and to be expected.

Jonathan desperately needed time to cocoon. He needed to just relax and acknowledge that he was in transition, and that it was important that he allow everything to settle before he even tried to move on.

After he allowed himself some space, he then could start to look for new ways of living his life. He needed a new strategy for creating his new life and finding his niche in Mexico.

Almost by definition, people who are brave enough to relocate to another country are rebels at heart, or at the very least, pioneers. Jonathan needed to recognize that just by moving to a foreign land he was being courageous. He needed to pat himself on the back and relax into the changes.

What Story Are You Living By?

"So I say the way to find your myth is to find your zeal, to find your support and know what stage of life you're in."

Joseph Campbell

When we no longer have a story, or as Campbell calls it, a *myth* to live by, that has relevance and meaning for our current situation, we lose our way and end up lost in the forest like Jonathan.

Campbell says that not only do our personal myths break down from time to time, but our cultural myths are under threat as well. As we become multicultural, global, and less provincial, our old certainties are also disappearing.

"The myths tell you that if you engage the world in a certain way…you are under the protection of this, that, or the other god. That's the model. We don't have that today. Life has changed in form so rapidly that even the forms that were normal to think about in the time of my boyhood are no longer around…and everything is moving very, very fast. Today we don't have the stasis that is required for the formation of a mythic tradition."

Carl Jung first used the term *myth* to describe the archetypal stories that guide our lives; Jung said getting to know the myth he lived by was his "task of tasks".

The term myth is used here to mean a story that points to inner truths we all experience as human beings. It does not mean something that isn't true, but just the opposite, something that is deeply true and part of our nature.

In the 1960s we smashed through the mythic traditions of the day. So now we lack stasis.

Lost on the Freeways of Texas

My roles while living in England had been wife, mother, and professional business trainer. My main role was clear; it was bringing up my kids, and earning a livelihood came second. A lesser role was advancing my career and my professional identity. That was my story. I was a wife and working mother living in a foreign country. I was an American living in Britain. My life was edgy and challenging.

Then, when all the changes happened and I moved to Houston I hit a wall! I had no roles anymore! There was a black hole where there used to be a whole host of activities and responsibilities. I was no longer a wife, my kids had grown up and left home, and I wasn't working. I no longer had the identity of being a foreigner and the distinction that gave me. This was a perfect prescription for crisis. I no longer knew who I was or my proper place in the world.

I had no story.

My identity was all in the past. How does one live in Houston? After the charming coziness of England, Houston seemed like a big wasteland of freeways and shopping malls, where everyone lived in their cars. I felt alienated and completely lost.

Drifting into the sunset, lost on the freeways.

I urgently needed to create a new story to live by—or die trying.

Does Your Story Work For You?

Your life story may resemble a myth or legend. Are you a *Hero* on an odyssey? Or are you a *Damsel in Distress*? I've heard people say they felt like they were living in a Greek tragedy. Does your life resemble a Shakespearean play? A fairy tale?

Finish this sentence: *My life is like…*

Whether it reminds you of a myth or legend isn't important. What is crucial is that you have a story to live by that makes sense of your life right now.

Your story guides your life, gives it meaning and gives you goals that you are working towards. Without a *relevant, up-to-date* story you cannot have passion for life.

When we were hippies we had a story—we were members of a counter-culture that was changing the world. We were part of a tribe. The identity was clear and the script exciting and compelling ...OK, a little crazy and irresponsible too. But it was risky and courageous at the same time.

The important thing to remember is that your story needs revising and updating as you approach each new stage in your life. If you don't revise it you can lose your way. You can become frustrated, lacking in inspiration and with no interest in your goals. Major changes can suddenly sweep away your roles, and with them your sense of identity.

Joseph Campbell compares our myth to a mask that we wear, and asks:

"This is the mystery of life and its masks. What're you going to do when the thing breaks, and it starts winding down? Are you just going to become an old dog getting older and older, sinking back into your body? Or, in the moment of the full moon have you made the jump to the solar light?"

Put Out To Pasture

What is our story about 'growing old'? Let's visit some of the different myths for aging that we Baby Boomers have to choose from— that were created in previous eras.

One is the theme of being *put out to pasture* at retirement age, and then shunted into a retirement village when we can no longer care for ourselves. In this scenario we spend our twilight years out of sight from the rest of society, mixing socially only with our own age group and having all responsibilities and daily chores taken care of. The result is often that one is reduced to a child-like dependent state, kept quiet with bridge games, outings and bingo, looking forward to ill-health, drug dependency and death. What fun.

In the meantime the unspoken message is—you are absolutely of no use to society anymore. Your age precludes that. Old age makes you totally irrelevant. Keep yourself entertained with childish activities until your time is up.

As the song goes, "*It ain't me, babe...*"

Ok, Ok, I know many people absolutely love retirement villages and they can be a godsend for some. To each his own. I know they are improving all the time and some are quite pleasant. It's just the idea of having that to look forward to fills me with *fear and loathing*. I guess it's not my time for it.

Another myth is the far more attractive one common among indigenous peoples, traditional cultures, and Catholic countries with large families. The old person becomes the *Elder*, the grandparent who lives with the family, shares responsibilities for bringing up the children, and taking on the role of advising the young.

While this is a much more appealing option, for those of us with families separated by long distances, this role is simply not feasible. This option works in societies where people live in the same place all their lives. Many of us don't do that anymore. We Baby Boomers have become global villagers with families spread out over different continents.

I don't know about you, but I'm not ready to *embrace my Elder*. Not just yet anyway. I'm also not crazy about taking on the *Crone's* role. Sounds old, post-menopausal, and terribly unsexy. Embracing your elder or crone doesn't necessarily feel like acceptance to me; it feels like throwing in the towel.

Rebel Against This!

A paradigm is a "framework containing the basic assumptions, ways of thinking, and methodology that are commonly accepted by members of a community or society".

We need new paradigms for aging that take into account healthy, active, still working, *rebellious* older people, who have no intention of being put out to pasture at any age.

Unfortunately, we have few dynamic role models to show us the way, and so once again we *Old Hippies* are on our own and making up the rules as we go. We need to bring that *Free Spirit* out of retirement in order to challenge the ideas being foisted on us. We need to rebel against being pressured into doing things we don't feel OK with, or are unhappy about.

To reiterate what we are up against:

—Every day, we are under pressure to take certain medications, simply because we're getting older. The drug companies would like us to be on drugs at every stage of our lives, from the cradle to the grave. Rebel against this!

—We are under pressure to move into retirement villages when are still reasonably young and active. We are under emotional blackmail to do this otherwise we will be a 'burden' to our loved ones. We are told to do it now before it's too late. Rebel against this!

—We are under pressure to retire at 65, whether we want to or not, and give way to younger people—losing the opportunity to share our wisdom and experience. Rebel against this!

—We are pressured to undergo plastic surgery in order to stay young looking and sexy. Men are pressured to take viagra so they can 'perform' like they did at 20 and be able to have a young partner. Older women feel like they are discarded. Rebel against this!

Rebel and then make up your own mind. Don't give into it. You aren't a sheep, you're a fully functioning adult human being. By all means take the drugs, move into the village, and have plastic surgery—but only if you want to. And just be aware that somebody is making a lot of money by keeping you scared.

I haven't had any surgery—I don't like needles or operations or cutting. A 'friend' the other day asked if I had "had any work done". I said no. She said, "well don't leave it too long. You're nice looking. It would be a shame to lose that."

I don't need, want, or welcome that kind of comment, meant to shame me into feeling like I must look 10 years younger than I am, and that I will somehow be left behind if I don't buckle down and get surgery. Face the inevitable! Stop trying to fight it! She and I never did develop a friendship …for some reason.

I have nothing against people choosing plastic surgery; I just resent it when anyone tries to make those who don't choose that route feel old and self conscious. I found out later that my 'friend' got a cut (pun intended) from the local plastic surgeon if she sent a referral.

The challenge is to create a new way to live, and to age, which makes us feel good about ourselves and our choices. And I want to do it my way.

Let's Review

If you are in transition shock and don't know which way to turn, it's important to stop and take stock of where you are and how you got there. It's time to cocoon. Do nothing, make no decisions, and don't try to figure out your goals. Take as long as you need to reorient yourself. Veg out for awhile.

Recognize that being in transition feels like being lost in a deep forest with no apparent way out.

While it's normal to feel panicky, panic can be dangerous; you can make some bad decisions while in panic mode and fall into that ditch. Relax and recognize that where you are is not only natural, it is part of the process of making big life transitions and evolving.

Acknowledging that you are in 'transition shock' is the first step to finding your way out of the situation you are in.

And the exciting bit is you get to write a new script for living that fits your new circumstances.

Think about this

How would you describe your current role or story in life?

How is this story working for you?

What would be a better one?

Write down your thoughts. Have fun with this—it's not meant to be deadly serious.

Now, let's go repair that compass and find our way of the forest. Let's find out how to make that *"jump to the solar light"*.

Chapter 3

"There are Places I Remember...": Grief—the Hidden Dragon

"Though I know I'll never lose affection
For people and things that went before
I know I'll often stop and think about them...in my life..."

The Beatles

Are you grieving or longing for something that you are missing but you can't quite identify? You can't even name what you have lost—it's just a sort of generalized feeling of unease, of loss, of sadness—a hole that needs filling. You feel like you have unfinished business that has to be seen to, but you can't quite pinpoint what it is. You are looking back.

Before you can move forward, you have to let go of the past. Otherwise you become like *Lot's Wife* fleeing the burning city of Sodom. She hesitated, looked back, and it was all over for her.

*"But Lot's wife behind him looked back,
and she became a pillar of salt."*

Genesis 19

One interpretation of the message from Lot's wife to us from across the centuries is that you and I can become pillars of salt—rigid and lifeless—if we look back on anything with longing, regret, or grief. It's fine to look back and remember and enjoy your memories. We all do that. The problems come when we constantly wish we could return to the past.

The number one reason people get stuck *is because they are grieving* and don't even realize it. Clinging to what is over, dead, or gone forever will prevent any progress in your life.

In the Greek myth, Demeter's daughter Persephone is kidnapped by the Lord of the Underworld, Hades. Demeter goes mad with grief looking for her; tearing her hair out, and wandering around distractedly. She becomes obsessed with trying to find her lost child but has no idea where to look.

Are you searching for something you have lost? Is it driving you to distraction? Is it your youth, your old career, your children living at home with you, or your friends and social circle in your old town?

Demeter's story can be a metaphor for anything lost that we can't find—and we don't even know what we are looking for.

Lot's wife needed to get to safety first. Then she would have time to remember the past and grieve for it. But she could never go back. Her old life was utterly destroyed in the fire and brimstone. Demeter eventually got her daughter Persephone back, but Persephone had changed forever from the experience. In the same way we can glean the good from our past, but we can never go back, and things will never be exactly the same. So we absolutely, no question about it, must, let it go.

Katherine's Never Ending Story...

I met Katherine years ago at a seminar in England. She was an attractive, 40ish lady, who within 5 minutes of meeting her, began to tell me her story.

Years before she had been married to a much younger man, whom she adored. He was a handsome chiropractor and she enjoyed working with him as his assistant in their successful clinic. They were good together and she loved her life. One day, out of the blue, he calmly announced that he was leaving Katherine for a much younger woman. He told her he had fallen in love with this woman and planned to start a family with her.

Katherine was devastated. Her heart was broken and she couldn't accept that he had left her for someone intellectually and socially inferior. Furthermore, they had discussed the subject of children before they got married and he had seemed fine with not having them.

What had happened? She felt betrayed and angry. To her it seemed obvious that he had lied about having children. She also felt old and abandoned. In her mind she went over and over their life together, trying to figure out where it had gone wrong.

Although this had happened years before, she still had tears in her eyes when she spoke about him. She clung to the hope that he would get tired of his new wife and would realize how shallow and inferior she was compared to Katherine. She lived for the day he would come back to her and beg her forgiveness. She followed their lives with an unhealthy interest.

I met Katherine on and off through the following years and each time she told her story as if it had just happened. The perpetual Katherine story, never changing, never evolving. Katherine couldn't move on, couldn't settle on her career, and couldn't find a new mate. Not surprising. Her story is unfortunately an archetypal one and she is a classic, tragic example of the need to let go of the past in order to move on to the future.

A shaman would say that Katherine had lost a fragment of her soul to the underworld when she experienced the shock of losing her beloved husband. Just like Demeter, she was crazed with grief over her loss. And the shaman would offer to take her on a journey of soul retrieval.

However, I suspect that Katherine would never agree to such a journey because she was clinging so tightly to the past. In a strange way she enjoyed her pain and her story. It gave her a myth to live by; the abandoned and betrayed wife, forever condemned to pine for her lost love. It may have been painful, but it was *her* story.

She couldn't face the truth that he had moved on and she needed to as well. It was more comforting to live in the past and cling to denial. She didn't want a new story.

I imagine you have met people like Katherine. She is an extreme case, but there are many people like her who refuse to face their current reality. Is this you? If you are stuck and feel like you are spinning your wheels, could it be that there is a part of you clinging to an old story— that you need to grieve and let go of?

Why Do We Cling?

There are many reasons why we cling to the past. William Bridges, in his book *Transitions*, says that when things fall apart in our lives and we are forced into transition, our whole sense of identity is threatened. We no longer know who we are—we *were* this person and *now* we are someone different.

Any major change can threaten our story and lead to disenchantment, disillusionment, dis-identification, and disorientation, according to Bridges. Job loss, divorce, death, ill health, or kids leaving home are great examples of events that can undermine our sense of who we are.

Change is painful. Even good change. Just ask anyone trying to give up smoking. So in order to avoid this pain we cling desperately to the old ways, the old habits, the old story. And we make excuses for our clinging.

Every change is like a mini-death; a death of the old.

It feels safer sometimes to live in the past instead of the present, so we hang on to old achievements, out of date relationships, redundant labels, and previous roles. This somehow lessens our confusion over where we fit in now. *I used to be great at my job! I used to have an exciting and important career! I used to earn a lot of money! I used to be so cool and radical!*

Have you ever met someone who constantly talks about what they accomplished in the past or how important they were *back then*? You can guarantee that they aren't doing anything relevant or exciting in the present.

I knew someone, an *Old Hippie* for sure, who had been editor, in New York, back in the 60s, of the iconic counter-culture paper, The *Village Voice.* This was her claim to fame, her glory days. She had been hip and at the cutting edge of the cultural revolution going on at the time. The problem was, every time you met with her, she would somehow insinuate this information into the conversation. The first time she told me, I thought it was pretty impressive; the second and third times I realized she was just boring.

We Baby Boomers and *Old Hippies* can easily fall into this trap. We can cling to past identities without bringing what we learned from them into our present lives. It's great that you have a past that was exciting, successful, and fun.

Now, what did you learn from it and how are you going to incorporate it into what you are doing now?

Why Do We Fear Change?

Change is threatening because it propels us from the known and predictable into the unknown. It reminds us of death, and we don't like to think about death, the *Big Kahuna* of change. We cling to life and the known and fear the unknown.

Pema Chodron in her book, *When Things Fall Apart*, says:

"...most of the time, warding off death is our biggest motivation...Time is passing. It's as natural as the seasons changing and day turning into night. But getting old, getting sick, losing what we love—we don't see those events as natural occurrences. We want to ward off that sense of death, no matter what."

Death, change, loss, and growing older *are* natural occurrences. But in modern life we are somehow cut off from this acceptance of nature taking its course— in many ways more cut off than our ancestors were. We want everything to be perfect and consider ourselves failures when things go wrong. But change isn't wrong— it's natural and inevitable.

We are largely alienated from nature and the natural cycles of life. And we have lost our rituals for segueing easily from season to season, age to age, from change to change.

So it's not surprising that we consider aging a failure. We want a pill, an operation, or a technology to put it right. Is there a hormone I can take? Stem cells? We are willing to pay someone to do whatever it takes to make this aging thing go away.

Moving On

The good news is, it doesn't have to be this way. It's possible to grieve for what was lost, and release the past; no matter how glorious and fun it was, or how much pain you endured. It's called moving on. But some people, like Katherine, deep down love their pain because it gives them a sense of identity. And others feel they must cling to the past to show how much they loved it.

—Moving on after the death, or loss, of a loved one doesn't mean you didn't love that person or that the relationship was a failure. Celebrate what was good instead of the pain. *Hey, we lasted 15 years!*

—Moving on from an old job doesn't mean you didn't learn a lot and accomplish some amazing things. Even getting fired doesn't necessarily mean it was all a waste of time. Let it go and focus on what's ahead. *Remember the old cliche that when the universe shuts one door, another one opens.*

—Relocating to another town or country doesn't mean you didn't enjoy where you lived before or that the move is a failure because you miss your old friends. *Accept that you miss them and get excited about meeting new people.*

—Being relieved when the kids *finally* leave home doesn't mean you didn't love being a parent and no longer want to be involved with your children's lives. Keep in touch and reboot your life. *Wow, what can you do now that that stage of your life has passed?*

So acknowledge the good about who or what you lost, and glean what you learned from it. Always look for what has opened up in your life as a result of your losses. This is such an important step in letting go and releasing your grief. There is something positive to be learned from every situation, every loss.

Accept that trials and tribulations are the price you pay for living an interesting life.

There are great things about growing older. People tend to focus and obsess on losses and ignore that there is actually a slew of valuable gains—wisdom, perspective, growth, not caring what people think, finally doing only what you want to do—to name just a few. Focus on this and not the loss.

The Importance of Ritual

So we need to grieve and we need to do it in a conscious way. Rituals have been around since the beginnings of mankind, for a good reason. They help us feel like a part of the ongoing process of life. When a baby is born we welcome it with baptism; when we find our life partner, we get married; when someone dies, we have a funeral.

However, we have lost many other less important rituals that acknowledged significant events in our lives. Traditional societies have more rituals to help with the many transitions of life. They are more in touch with the cycles of nature.

Go and live in a Latin American country for awhile if you don't believe me. Every other week there is a saint's day with fireworks, parades, and pilgrimages, celebrating some archetypal aspect of life. It reminds people of their heritage and that they are not alone, but part of the human tribe. Life is ongoing and change happens.

Rituals help us place ourselves in relation to our past and future.

In modern life our mileposts are different. We change jobs, relationships, countries and even religions far more often than people did in the past or in simpler societies. Why don't we have rituals for these events? We need them. So it's good to make up your own rituals—a great example is a farewell party when someone is moving away.

Without formal rites of passage to signify our transitions many of us don't even realize we are grieving or need to let go.

We don't grieve for a lost job—or do we?

We don't grieve when we move to another city, or to another country—or do we?

We don't grieve when we realize we are no longer young—or do we?

We don't grieve when that divorce finally comes through—do we?

Yes we do! We often just don't have effective methods to recognize these losses and to help us through the transition period; to grieve and accept and let them go. We need to feel part of something larger than ourselves, part of the human race.

Instead, we head to the gym or book a facelift. Worse, we have a drink or take an antidepressant to suppress those natural feelings of loss, and to numb the pain.

New Rituals for Letting Go

If you recognize that you are having difficulty letting go of something in your past, it's good to **write about** what you are grieving. Writing it down helps uncover the real emotions you are feeling.

Sadness, grief, and pain can sometimes be a cover for resentment, anger, guilt and fear. It is important to find the real emotions.

Next, it's good to **acknowledge what was great** about the person or circumstance in your life that is now over and gone. It could be a relationship that has ended—what was good about it? How did it make you a better person for the experience? It could be a job you've lost—what did you enjoy about it and what did you learn?

It could be your old life as a whole—like mine when I moved from England to Texas. Oh boy, did I miss England and my old life. But it was hard for me to admit it, because that would imply I had made a mistake in moving. So instead I went into denial.

Sometimes when we are in denial, we have a tendency to *demonize* what we have lost in order to justify our choices or to feel better about having lost it. This doesn't honor it nor help us let go. *Your ex-partner wasn't really a demon. Your old boss probably wasn't Hitler. It didn't rain all the time in England!*

And just as unhelpful is to **idealize** what was lost. Your old life was fabulous and you were so happy back then. Sure it was. Sure you were. Your children were perfect and you adored being a stay-at-home parent. That is probably not totally true either.

This can be especially true of chronic complainers—they moan non-stop about their situation, and then when it's in the past, talk about how wonderful it was. Meanwhile, their friends tear their hair out.

So **write about the good and the bad and describe whatever emotions you are feeling.** Give yourself permission to fully experience these emotions. It's all OK. The important thing is to be honest about what you are feeling.

(Some emotions or losses are too painful to be OK with. This is not about trivializing tragedy. In cases of overwhelming sorrow, seeking help and support is the best thing to do.)

Share Your Loss

It is essential to find someone to **share your emotions** with. This could be a coach, a spiritual leader, or a trusted friend. Tell them that you need them to help you to let go of something holding you back from moving on in life. All they need to do is listen. Share the good and the bad and all the emotions you are feeling. Let yourself grieve for what is over and lost.

You may need to do this more than once. That's OK. Just don't get stuck in the victim mode like my friend Katherine.

I know of people who share their losses by inviting several close friends out to lunch on a regular basis where they all discuss what's going on in their lives and what they need to release. A mini-tribe.

In the case of loss of a loved one, or something deeply wounding, you may need to do the sharing more than once. Some things take more time and you can't rush it.

If it feels appropriate, make up your own rituals for letting go and saying good-bye. You can burn symbolic objects, such as old photos or mementos, in a fire, or simply design your very own *farewell ceremony* to take place during the full moon. This can be done alone or with friends. Light a candle, build a fire, talk about what you are releasing, and say goodbye.

I Missed My Old Career

After I left England I unknowingly started grieving for my old career that had been arbitrarily cut short by my move to Houston, and then to Mexico. I thought I could recreate my career anywhere, but when I tried to set up my practice outside of England, I couldn't get my business off the ground.

I didn't have the old drive, the old enthusiasm. When I did make appointments I just felt dread. What was the matter? I still had my skills and experience and I knew how to practice as a coach and therapist. I knew I was pretty darn good at what I did. However, what I lacked was motivation and interest. And what had previously been exciting and challenging now felt like a burden.

The turning point for me was when I realized it was simply grief that was making me feel the way I did. I hadn't reckoned on how much I would miss my old colleagues in England who had trained with me and whom I used to meet with every week to discuss our work. I hadn't realized how much I would miss the status I enjoyed working in a well-known clinic where the owner, a highly successful therapist, had invited me to work. I had been flattered and it had jumpstarted my career. I missed that prestige and the buzz of working in a busy clinic.

Working from my little casita in my garden in Mexico wasn't the same. It was lonely, for starters. I had no one to bounce ideas off, nor consult with about clients. I wanted to shout out to everyone how successful and fun and terrifically exciting my career had been in England, but fortunately stopped myself because of how pathetic that would sound, just like the lady who used to edit the *Village Voice*. Who cares? Trust me, *nobody* is interested in what you did in the past. People are only interested in what you are now, not what you were.

It was only when I regaled my coach with my story, and then created my own ritual to say goodbye to my past career, that I was able to let go. Having someone listen to me talk about my old career without yawning or falling asleep was therapeutic. I had been so reluctant to mention it to anybody. Now I could express all the longings, regrets, and even brag about the accomplishments and successes I had had and lost —without feeling self conscious.

I had been full of regret and was constantly looking back, like Lot's wife. I needed to get out of denial and face the questions I had been avoiding. *Had I made the right decision to leave England? Could I ever go back? Would it be possible to go back and take up where I had left off?*

Once I faced these questions it was like a huge release to me. I realized I couldn't go back even if I wanted to. Everyone there had made changes too and half my old friends were no longer even living in England. Even if I could, I wouldn't really want to take up where I had left off. I actually *had* moved on; I just needed to acknowledge it. My decision to leave was right for me at that time and I began to come to terms with it and stopped beating myself up.

What could I glean from this? I had my skills and my experience, but I couldn't recreate my *old* career. I needed to create a *new* one that was based on the old and that took advantage of all the experience and valuable skills I had developed. But it wasn't going back—it was moving forward.

The past no longer existed and I had made choices. I finally made peace with my past. You can do this too.

De-cluttering—a Great Ritual

I discovered that clutter is stuff from the past and replicates the state of your mind.

I had plenty of clutter. De-cluttering is a great ritual for letting go.

A cluttered environment can hold you back as much as your cluttered mind. Clutter in your home or office will clog up your spirit and keep you from focusing on the present.

The next step after talking about my past was to physically let it go. When I uncluttered my office and threw out my old files and notes which represented my past career, it felt really good. I created little ceremonies for saying good-bye to all my old stuff as I threw it out. Of course I kept many books and manuals— not everything went in the trash. I can't say it was easy— making decisions about what to keep and what has to go can be really difficult.

For me, de-cluttering, cleaning out, was another turning point, a new beginning. It was only when I had clear spaces around me that I was able to start figuring out what I really wanted to do in my new life.

So clear out those drawers, closets and bookshelves. The stuff in them represents the past. Clutter will forever hold you back and anchor you in the past.

Sasha—Un-cluttering Her Thinking

Sasha was approaching 50— she was non-conformist, larger than life, and had an outgoing personality. She badly needed to change her work situation. She was self-employed, in her own business of designing websites. But, although she called it a business, she was actually working freelance and on call all hours. She was stressed, overworked, woefully underestimating how long jobs would take, and under-charging. Clients took advantage of her, worked her hard and then were slow to pay.

She dreamed of being able to retire, or at the very least take a few months off now and then, but that was impossible with her current work habits. She was living hand to mouth.

Sasha needed to let go of her old way of doing things and redesign her business if she had any hope of living her dream. But she was clinging to the familiar, the habitual. Designing websites had worked in the past. It wasn't working now. But she found it was comfortable to do what she had always done. Isn't it always?

Eventually with coaxing from me, her coach, she recognized that the old ways had to change. She had to let go of old habits of thinking that weren't working for her. She had to de-clutter her mind and her working environment and push away from the familiar before she could start afresh.

After struggling with letting go of her old work habits, she eventually became energized with the idea of revamping her business so that she could make money from training and writing, as well as from web design. She started organizing her time so she could start writing her book.

The principle of letting go and de-cluttering applies to any situation where you feel stuck or where what you are doing *just isn't working for you anymore.*

Let's Review

We have to let go of the past before we can move on to the future.

Letting go is about grieving. It involves acknowledging what was good and what was bad.

Moving on involves harvesting what we want to bring with us and releasing what we no longer need.

Writing in a journal helps to let go of emotions and thinking patterns that are no longer serving us.

Sharing your grief or loss with a trusted friend or coach is enormously helpful.

It's important to de-clutter your personal space. Clutter is stuff from the past and reflects the state of your mind.

We need to create rituals that acknowledge transitions and treat them with the respect they deserve.

Ask Yourself This

Am I grieving for something from my past? Old friends and activities, a job or career, a place I used to live?

What old ideas or ways of doing things do I need to let go of so I can move on?

What would help me to let go?

You may need to talk this over with someone, or perform some sort of ritual. Or, just being aware of what is going on inside may be enough for you to move on.

You are now ready to set out on your journey— your *Hero's Journey*! You have prepared for the journey by acknowledging where you are right now, and climbing out of the hole of denial. You have taken steps to let go and grieve for the past, which has been holding you back. You have uncluttered your environment and your thinking, and you're starting to feel better already.

You have already faced a giant dragon, which is grief for the past. Now it's time to *go forth* and face the rest of the dragons that are lurking in the shadows and may try to prevent you from finding your treasure. Are you feeling brave? Bring it on!

Keep that hippie van moving—the trip is going to get more exciting…

Chapter 4

"Hello Darkness, My Old Friend...": Entering the Caves of Your Subconscious Dragons

"In the struggle of primitive man to achieve consciousness this conflict is expressed by the contest between the archetypal hero and the cosmic powers of evil, personified by dragons and other monsters."

Joseph Henderson—*Ancient Myths and Modern Man*

It's time to start your journey, your Hero's Journey to find your place in life after getting hit by some knockout transitions. You have faced the hidden dragon—grief for the past—but you are still reeling and dizzy and full of fear about the future. In theory you want to face it fearlessly and rebelliously, but right now you're still licking your wounds.

You're not even sure you want to take a journey...metaphorical or not. Dangers and challenges await you and some of it might be a little unpleasant. You are going to have to fight some battles along the way.

So, why take this journey at all? It sounds uncomfortable and dangerous— meeting dragons and stirring up dark forces within. Facing that first dragon was hard enough. Why not just stay on the couch, switch on the TV, and ignore this call?

The consequences of not taking this journey and facing your fears are that you may never become authentic and find your true voice. You may never find your purpose, what you are here for. You may never find what your unique contribution to life can be. It's time to do it now!

That's pretty compelling. Come on. This journey is actually going to be worth it. You simply must first face the things lurking in the caverns of your mind.

Carol Pearson, in her book *Awakening The Heroes Within*, says if we avoid the call to confront our terrors that lie hidden in myth "we miss our connection to life's intensity and mystery. Finding our own connection with such eternal patterns provides a sense of meaning and significance in even the most painful or alienated moments and in this way restores nobility to life."

You have stopped and acknowledged where you are; in the deep dark forest of transition, and that you are feeling lost and disoriented. You want to find your way out and start your search for meaning. Your goal is to age with purpose and courage and to live the rest of your life authentically.

Now it's time to enter those caves and confront your dragons.

Dragon Caves

"You must enter the cave you fear most," said my Coach.

"No. That subject is off limits. I won't go there!" I replied.

"You must face your worst fears. If you don't learn how to fight your dragons, how can you help your clients?" he said.

You are very afraid of that cave you see over there. Dark things lurk in it and you are worried they could prove to be very unpleasant.

Dragons live in that cave and you don't want to stir them up. You prefer that they stay sleeping. Let sleeping dragons lie, you think.

Dragons are those fears and negative beliefs that lie hidden in the dark corners of your subconscious mind, the cave or dungeon. The last thing you feel like doing is stirring them up and forcing them out into the light of day. You prefer them out of sight. You've worked very hard to keep them in that cave; it has involved denial, stuffing down emotions, and repression. Keeping dragons in their caves takes a lot of energy.

Let's go dragon chasing. Don't worry, you're in your trusty van—and safe. We can slay them, tame them, or make friends with them. But, as long as they stay in the cave they have power to make us unhappy, stuck, frustrated—and worst of all, scared.

There are many different types of dragons. On this part of the journey together we will confront a few of the most common dragons:

—**negative emotions**

—**limiting beliefs**

—**bad habits and addictions.**

Negative Emotions—Lurking in the Corners of Your Mind

Negative emotions are powerful dragons: fear, grief, despair, guilt, regret and anger. They lurk inside memories from the past, sometimes from early youth, and can influence your behavior all the way into old age. They are careful not to be caught or confronted and stay under the radar most of the time. You become so used to them that you don't even know they are there.

You can become aware of them if you sometimes fall into rage at a slight provocation, not realizing at first that it stems from an event that occurred forty years ago. Have you ever felt sad or angry for no obvious reason? It could have been triggered by anything—a car going past, a scent, a song—that reminds you subconsciously of someone in the distant past. That's a dragon.

Negative emotions can seriously impact your life and make you unhappy. They can blindside you, take you by surprise, and ruin your day.

Have you experienced fear, anxiety or dread for the future? Do you ever fear being alone? You can never be joyous and upbeat as long as you are victim to these emotions. They will eat into any positive thoughts you have and overpower them.

Limiting beliefs—they must be true?

Limiting beliefs are the second type of dragon. They are the thought patterns that go hand in hand with negative emotions. A belief is *that which we hold to be true*. So a limiting belief is something we hold to be true about ourselves *that is inherently disempowering.*

You are either taught limiting beliefs, or you learn them from negative experiences. Most of them are installed before age 7 when we are especially vulnerable to the opinions of others.

At a young age, we have no filters that enable us to reject negative remarks. A teacher criticizing your abilities in a certain area can affect you in that subject for life. You don't even realize it was just one person's passing opinion, meaning nothing, which has affected you for years. Dragon alert!

We are especially prone to taking on our parents' limiting beliefs:

Our family has never done anything like this (so who do you think you are?)

Nobody in our family has ever made money (and I doubt you will be the first).

You never were good at athletics, just like me (do you think you're better than I am?)

Well, I don't think math is your subject. Most girls aren't good at it (it's not feminine).

The list goes on. What were the limiting beliefs in your family? While it's better to focus on the empowering beliefs, it can be illuminating and liberating to uncover the limiting ones.

And likewise, when it comes to aging, we take on the beliefs we have been shown and taught.

You're too old to do that (you're making a fool of yourself).

It's not age appropriate (you look like mutton dressed as lamb).

It's important to age "gracefully" (tone that down and act your age!)

It's too late to live your dream (accept reality).

Once you hit 50 it's downhill from there on (give up now and save yourself stress).

What are the role models in your family for aging? Do they work for you? Inspire you? Give you courage for growing older? Or do they limit you? It's probably a mix of both.

My Parents

I had amazing parents—kind, intelligent and loving. They were wonderful role models in many areas of my life. Yet their models for aging don't work for me.

My Father

My father was a Presbyterian preacher from the Deep South, a wonderful southern gentleman of the old school; a Christian liberal with compassionate social beliefs, kind of a rarity these days.

As retirement approached, he became more and more unhappy. He saw the other retired preachers playing golf, and that became his metaphor for retirement—the Golf Syndrome—his equivalent to being put out to pasture. He didn't like golf much and it seemed to him to be a waste of time.

He wondered aloud where he would funnel all his reading and studying, which he loved to do so much. As a preacher it had always provided fodder for his sermons. It had a purpose.

Two weeks after he retired he saw a job advertised in Kathmandu, Nepal, for a two-year stint running an international church. He got the job and off they went—my rather untraveled and naïve parents— to the Himalayas.

He dropped dead from heart failure six months into the two-year stint. The extremely high altitude of the Himalayas, plus the strange food and unhygienic water, proved too much for his heart.

What went wrong? He had tried to reinvent himself, to create a new story. The problem was he didn't give himself time to cocoon, to transition, before he set off on his adventure. He was still in transition shock from retiring when he arrived in Kathmandu.

If he had given himself the needed time to wander in the forest a bit, to reflect and decide on what he really wanted, he might have seen another possibility for retirement; one where he would have certainly been in demand as a guest preacher. He and my mother could have traveled the country and he could have indulged his love for preaching without the responsibilities of running a church. Shame. He let dread of the golf course force a panicky decision that proved fatal.

This showed me that we need time to cocoon, to wander, and to reflect before we make life-changing decisions. It also taught me the importance of tempering our impulses with common sense. If we allow them, things fall into place of their own accord and we can rewrite our stories with ease.

We panic in the forest, but sometimes it's good to just rest there a while.

My Mother

So my mother was widowed at the early age of 65. She had lived a full life as a preacher's wife and then became a widow and grandmother. She embraced the widow's role and coasted into old age.

In her 70s she moved into a retirement village where she set about filling her time. She joined in church activities, saw her children, grandchildren, and friends, and did a little artwork. She passed away peacefully at age 93. This was her life; it worked for her and she was happy, and but it wasn't a model that appealed to me much.

So I was left with two ways that I did not want to age. Although I admired my father's spirit of adventure, I didn't want to drop dead at age 65. I also couldn't see myself in a retirement village, drifting into the sunset. Neither of these models fit my belief that life can be passionate and full of juice into a very old age.

They didn't fit very well with the *Old Hippie* in me. Caveat: I reserve the right to change my mind on this one at a later date!

I needed to slay these dragons of limiting beliefs if I wanted to age with passion and rebellion.

The options for aging are limitless; don't give up until you find one that suits you.

Bad Habits and Addictions—Very Dangerous Dragons

Our third type of dragon is that of bad habits and addictions. Habits are automatic, unconscious behaviors. We couldn't live very well if our unconscious mind *didn't* form habits—we would have to relearn everything anew each time we took an action.

Brushing our teeth, driving a car, making a cup of tea—these are habits. We don't have to think about them when we do them. These are learned, unconscious behaviors.

However, sometimes bad habits form and can be very hard to break.

Bad habits can be formed around food, drugs, cigarettes and alcohol. These are self-destructive habits and can kill us if we let them. Dangerous dragons. Other bad habits are subtler, such as too much Internet, television, shopping or gambling. They won't actually kill us, but they can suck our time and energy, and waste our lives.

Steven Pressfield, in his book, *The War of Art*, says procrastination should be included in this list:

"The most pernicious aspect of procrastination is that it can become a habit. We don't just put off our lives today; we put them off till our deathbed."

Procrastination is putting off what needs to be done. It's the constant mindset of *I'll do that another time*. The other time never comes. We especially tend to procrastinate on our goals. We keep delaying them until we don't even realize we are doing it and eventually we even forget about them.

Start noticing how you think about your goals. Are you continuously delaying getting started? If so, counter this with getting in the habit of taking immediate action on an idea.

The truth is, you cannot age with enthusiasm if you have an addiction or bad habit. It will undermine everything you try to do and will lurk in the back of your consciousness, just like a dangerous dragon lurking in a cave. Addictions are the dragons we are most reluctant to face; we will make all kinds of excuses to justify and keep them out of sight. We must face them, and fight them, however, if we want to live a satisfying and fulfilling life.

That which we defend most heatedly is usually a dragon. That food we insist we can't do without is usually the one causing problems. The politician who gets most agitated about gays is usually in the closet and in denial. You know the way it works.

But cigarettes help me relax! says almost every smoker.

The First Step in Dragon Taming

Dragon taming isn't so difficult when you know how, at least for the first two types of dragon—negative emotions and limiting beliefs. Addictions and bad habits are a little different and may take a bit more work to get rid of.

The first step is to go into the dragon's cave and shine a light around. Take a look at what's there. Chances are, once you face it squarely, the dragon will disappear. Dragons don't like the light of day.

Sebastian's Story—Drowning in Debt

Sebastian was a young man I met in England. He had a young family and one day found himself deeply in debt. He came to me for help because he felt humiliated and frightened by the threat of losing his flat because he couldn't pay the rent. He had borrowed against his credit card to pay the power bills.

As his debts accumulated he had started to put all his bills in a drawer, unopened.

The cave he needed to go in was that drawer. There the dragon of financial fear lurked. Until he went in that cave and acknowledged his true financial position he would never overcome his difficulties.

Once he opened the drawer, took out the bills, opened them up and evaluated where he was, his battle was halfway over. He was then able to find a financial mentor and get help.

Dragon harboring caves will keep appearing in your life. Get in the habit of entering them and shining the light of awareness around. That's frequently all you have to do. Make it a habit, a good habit. A big part of the success of Alcoholics Anonymous is that adherents are continually confronting their dragons.

You need to acknowledge the dragon. Awareness and honesty dissipate its power.

Like the *Wicked Witch of the West* who melted when water was thrown on her, some dragons melt with the water of awareness.

Let's Review

You are ready to begin your journey out of the forest, but first there are caves with dragons inside that need to be entered.

Caves represent your subconscious mind and dragons are anything subconsciously standing in the way of you finding your purpose and living a fulfilling life.

The most common dragons are negative emotions, limiting beliefs and bad habits. You must confront these dragons if you want to move on with your life and achieve your goals.

Usually just by entering the cave and shining the light of awareness around, you can defeat most dragons.

Discovering Your Dragons

Do you sometimes fall into rage at the slightest provocation? What provokes it?

Do you ever become sad for fearful for no obvious reason? When? What provokes it? Does it remind you of something?

Can you name a few of the limiting beliefs you have picked up from your early life?

What Caves to Enter?

What subjects are you most touchy about or reluctant to discuss?

What causes you to experience a negative emotion, such as sadness or anger, every time you think about it?

What are you most defensive about, get in arguments about?

Some dragons are really stubborn and may need an intervention. You may need to get tougher and slay these dragons. We'll look at how we can defeat these *stubborn dragons* in the next chapter. You're doing great! Let's forge ahead. Drive on!

Chapter 5

"Break on Through to the Other Side!":
Techniques for Slaying Dragons

"The very cave you are afraid to enter turns out to be the source of what you are looking for. The damned thing in the cave that was so dreaded has become the center."

Joseph Campbell

Dragons are anything preventing you from finding your purpose or becoming fulfilled and happy. They typically show up as negative emotions, limiting beliefs or bad habits and addictions. They sabotage your best intentions.

If the dragons lurking in the cave of your subconscious mind don't disappear easily simply by becoming aware of them, you may need to employ some help and use some sort of intervention.

As a Life Coach and Hypnotherapist, people frequently come to see me to release negative emotions and beliefs, and to change bad habits. Most clients have some sort of dragon residing inside, causing unhappiness.

I want to share with you in this chapter my favorite ways of taming, slaying or befriending them. In my experience these unconventional techniques are the most effective and easy to use.

Let me stress that these are coaching techniques and are not suitable for those who have serious mental illness: suicidal tendencies, deep depression, or uncontrollable mood swings. Coaching techniques are for the mentally stable person who has some issues.

EFT—The Tapping Method

Emotional Freedom Techniques (EFT) is an energy medicine intervention that involves lightly tapping on certain points on the body and head to release negative emotions and beliefs. It is simple, safe and can easily be self-administered.

EFT was developed by Gary Craig in the 1990s, is used to treat a wide variety of physical and psychological disorders, and especially focuses on stubborn emotional problems.

Gary Craig, the developer of EFT says that, "The cause of ALL negative emotions is a disruption in the body's energy system. This includes fears, phobias, anger, grief, anxiety, depression, traumatic memories, PTSD, worry, guilt and all limiting emotions in sports, business and the performing arts."

EFT uses the same ancient Chinese meridian system employed by acupuncture. Instead of using needles, EFT stimulates the same meridian points by tapping lightly on them with two or three fingers. While tapping on these points, you are encouraged to focus on the negative emotion or belief that is causing the problem. In this way the blockage is dispersed and the energy flows freely again.

By tapping on the energy points while thinking about the *negative* emotion you restore the balance in the energy system.

I use EFT for many issues and find it works quite miraculously.

Blood Tests!

I had to go to a clinic recently for a routine blood test.

I have had a long-standing phobia of needles and immediately went into panic mode. The tourniquet on the arm, bringing up the vein, the sight of the needle going in, just isn't OK with me. I became a babbling fool and couldn't hold my arm still.

I asked if I could go into another room for a few minutes to calm down. I began gently tapping on my panicky emotions. Ten minutes later I placidly walked back into the room and even laughed while the needle went in. Wow. Emotional rescue indeed.

I have had several blood tests since then, and can report that the panic has almost completely disappeared with that one session of tapping.

EFT is easy to learn, is quick, and it demonstrably works. It is becoming more and more accepted into mainstream thinking with well-known advocates such as Dr. Deepak Chopra, Dr. Bruce Lipton, Dr. Mercola and television's Dr. Oz, among its enthusiastic proponents. Practitioners of EFT number in the thousands and it is used worldwide. The technique is completely safe.

Instructions for EFT are all over the internet. You can find videos that you can follow along. I have included the basic technique here so that you can try it straight away.

The Basic Technique (With Thanks To Gary Craig)

EFT Tapping Points:

The Karate Chop point is located at the center of the fleshy part of the outside of your hand (either hand) between the top of the wrist and the base of the baby finger or....stated differently....the part of your hand you would use to deliver a karate chop.

Top of the head. If you were to draw a line from one ear, over the head, to the other ear, and another line from your nose to the back of your neck, the top of the head point is where those two lines would intersect.

Eyebrow. At the beginning of the eyebrow, just above and to one side of the nose.

Outside of the eye. On the bone bordering the corner of the eye.

Under the eye. On the bone under an eye about 1 inch below the pupil.

Under the nose. Between the bottom of your nose and the top of your upper lip.

Under the chin. Between the point of your chin and the bottom of your lower lip.

Collar Bone. The junction where the sternum (breastbone), collarbone and the first rib meet. To locate it, first place your forefinger on the U-shaped notch at the top of the breastbone (about where a man would knot his tie). From the bottom of the U, move your forefinger down toward the navel 1 inch and then go to the left (or right) 1 inch.

Under the arm. On the side of the body about 4 inches below the armpit.

Some of the tapping points have twin points on each side of the body. For example, the eyebrow point on the right side of the body has a twin point on the left side of the body.

You can switch sides when you tap these points.

The tapping is done with two or more fingertips.

You tap approximately 5 times on each point.

The process is easily memorized. After you have tapped the Karate Chop Point, the rest of the points go down the body. Start with the Top of the Head, then the Eyebrow Point, then the Side of the Eye, and so on down the body. End with Under the Arm.

The Steps:

1. Identify the issue: Make a mental note of what is troubling you. This becomes the target on which you focus the tapping.

For emotional issues you can recreate the memories in your mind and assess your discomfort. For physical ailments you can simply assess the existing pain or discomfort.

Only deal with one issue at a time. Do not tap on more than one at a time.

2. Rate the issue: Determine the intensity on a scale from 0 to 10, with 10 being terrible and 0 being nothing to bother about. You are looking for memories or discomfort that rates 5 and above with the aim of getting them below 5.

3. The Setup: The Setup is a process we use to start each round of tapping. It acknowledges the problem and affirms that you accept yourself even though you have it. Tap on the Karate Chop Point while saying;

"Even though I have this _____, I deeply and completely accept myself".

For example: "Even though I have this fear of needles and panic when I have blood tests, I deeply and completely accept myself."

Or, "Even though *I'm feeling really angry with my partner*, I deeply and completely accept myself."

Or, "Even though *I feel insecure at social events*, I deeply and completely accept myself."

The language that you use must always aim at the negative. This is essential because it is the negative that creates the energy disruptions that the tapping clears (and thus brings peace to the system). EFT needs to aim at the negative so it can be neutralized.

Do The Setup two times and then move on to The Sequence.

4. The Sequence: Tap each of the points 5 times while saying a Reminder Phrase that keeps your system tuned into the issue.

Top of the head - Eyebrow – Side of the eye – Under the eye – Under the nose – Under the chin – Collarbone – Under the arm

The Reminder Phrase is quite simple as you need only identify the issue with some brief wording. Depending on your issue, you might say the following at each tapping point:

This fear of needles…tap, tap, tap…

Or, *This anger…*

Or, *This insecurity…*

5. Test The Intensity Again: Finally, you establish an *after* level of the issue's intensity by assigning a number to it on a 0-

10 scale. You compare this with the *before* level to see how much progress you have made. If you are not down to zero then repeat the process until you either achieve zero, or a number low enough that it feels OK to live with.

I find I usually need to tap for at least 10 minutes, with about 10 rounds, to get the results I'm looking for. However, some people get results with one round.

I love to use this when I'm really mad or upset about something and can't talk myself out of it. My brain, along with any semblance of self control, has flown the coop. I think most people experience emotions they can't control at some point.

Cold Water!

I also can't stand getting into cold water. When I'm on vacation with my family this can be a problem when we are swimming. I stand at the edge, unable to put more than my big toe in the cold water, creating a huge drama of shivering and complaining, while everyone else is swimming happily. I use EFT— I tap for about 5 minutes on my intense dislike of cold water—and voila, I can then dive straight in. It works every time.

Although the examples I have given may seem relatively trivial, do not underestimate EFT. It can be incredibly effective for long-standing, serious issues that date from way back in the distant past but keep showing up in the present. These issues can be triggered by something that reminds us unconsciously of the past negative experience.

It has been proven especially helpful for war veterans and others suffering trauma, such as abuse or violence. Let me stress though, that anyone who has suffered abuse may want to consult a mental health professional.

EFT is an amazing weapon for fighting dragons—emotions, beliefs and habits that don't serve us.

Whenever you have an inappropriate emotional reaction to something, ask yourself when you have felt that emotion before. Keep going back until you get to an event at an early age. Then try tapping on that event and that emotion.

Hypnotherapy

Hypnotherapy is another excellent and well-established alternative method for eliminating bad habits. It's a real dragon chaser. I would rate it the most pleasant of the releasing and healing techniques available and it certainly is the easiest for the client. *You can just lie back and relax and listen to the sound of my voice...*

It is acknowledged by many to be the one of the best ways to quit smoking and for dealing with sugar addictions, soda addictions, overeating, fears and phobias.

Hypnosis can help you tap into the healing powers of your subconscious mind and address long standing health issues without drugs or surgery. I know, because it has worked for me in areas of my own health where both orthodox medicine and some other alternative methods failed me.

Headaches, heart arrhythmias, stomach problems, sleep problems—these are all issues that hypnosis can address.

How Does it Work?

Hypnosis is simply a deeply relaxed physical and mental condition called the trance state. The use of hypnosis for therapeutic purposes is referred to as hypnotherapy.

Practitioners of hypnotherapy believe that the subconscious mind holds the key to change. By inducing the trance state the therapist is able to communicate directly to the unconscious mind, which becomes more suggestible with relaxation. With trance the therapist bypasses the distractions of the conscious thinking mind and the client thereby becomes less resistant to change. Those dragons just float away in a happy stupor.

The sessions are pleasant and relaxing and most clients report feeling quite blissful for hours after. Clients enjoy it because it's effortless and easy for them.

There are several ways you can use hypnosis. One is with a hypnotherapist guiding you, helping you relax, and saying the affirmations for you. The other is self-hypnosis, which is similar to meditation, but differs in that you have an agenda for change. In self-hypnosis when you have relaxed completely you silently repeat to yourself affirmations for the desired improvements.

Guidelines For Affirmations to Use In Self-Hypnosis

Affirmations are positive statements that you make to yourself to assist achieving your goals. They can be said out loud or silently. They are statements of what you want to be true about yourself, and you state them as if they are already true.

Affirmations can be used to enhance goal achieving, to make changes, or to eliminate bad habits. They are effective dragon chasers.

It helps to write out your affirmations ahead of time. Here are some guidelines for affirmations:

1) **State your goal in the present tense**, as if it is already achieved. *I am X*...rather than *I will X* ... *I will* places your goal in the future and the danger is it may stay there.

2) **State your goal in positive language**. Do not focus on what you are trying to get rid of. State, *I am my ideal weight* rather than, *I am no longer fat*.

The unconscious mind processes in images, therefore the risk is, if you state the latter, it will visualize fat and create it.

The unconscious mind is keen to carry out our wishes so be careful what you tell it to do and what pictures you are creating for it.

3) **Make sure your goal is personal to you** and is not for someone else. Use lots of *I am...*, *I have...*, *or I allow myself...* statements. These statements avoid resistance or negative reactions.

I allow myself to learn Spanish easily and effortlessly.

I allow myself easily to achieve and maintain my ideal body weight.

I allow myself to sleep blissfully, straight through the night.

You can end your affirmation with statements such as, "*I am now instructing my unconscious mind to assist me in making these changes right now*". Robert Anthony, the personal development trainer and hypnotherapist, likes to finish with the command, "*Make it so!*" which he picked up from Star Trek.

Hypnotherapists use affirmations to imprint suggestions for change into the subconscious mind while the client is deeply relaxed and suggestible. When you used them in self-hypnosis, write them out ahead of time. You can memorize them and repeat them silently or you can record them yourself and play them while in the relaxed trance state.

You may also find that simply opening your eyes and reading them silently works perfectly well for you. It will not affect your relaxed state. When you are finished, simply close your eyes again.

In my opinion hypnosis works best with a hypnotherapist guiding you, at least for the first time. You can ask the hypnotherapist to teach you self-hypnosis.

Befriending Your Dragons

I mentioned earlier that we could tame slay, or befriend our dragons. Befriending them involves buying into the Jungian belief that everything we do, even seemingly negative behavior, has a positive intent.

This implies that dragons are really our teachers.

One way to disempower a dragon is to recognize its positive intent for you and negotiate with it to come to a compromise that allows you to let go of the negative behavior or emotion. The part of you driving the behavior, the dragon, needs reassurance that you have learned the lessons and that you are going to be safe in the future.

In NLP (Neuro-linguistic Programming) there is a technique known as *Parts Integration,* which aims to integrate opposing parts of you that seem to be driving conflicting behavior. I'm sure you've heard yourself say at times, *"part of me wants to go to the event, and part of me doesn't"*, or *"Part of me wants to stop smoking and part of me doesn't." "Part of me wants to get fit but part of me can't be bothered."*

We instinctively know we have parts that are sometimes are at odds with each other and that this causes internal conflict. The conflict can be a major cause of procrastination and stuck states. When you are battling yourself, you can't move.

In this technique you imagine bringing out the opposing parts on each hand— the part driving the bad behavior on one hand and the part that wants to change on the other— and getting the two to recognize and communicate with each other.

Parts Integration Technique

First clarify the unwanted behavior, emotion or limiting belief. Notice that there are two opposing forces or parts in you— a part that wants to change and a part that resists change. Identify the internal conflict.

1) Identify the parts in conflict and name each one. (E.g. the part of me that wants to smoke and the part that wants to quit.)

2) Locate one part on each hand. Rest one hand on each knee, palm facing upward.

3) Create a visual image on your palm, and focusing on one hand at a time ask:

What does it look like?

Does it remind me of anyone?

How is it dressed?

Who does it sound like?

When you have described one part fully, repeat the process for the other part, on the other hand.

4) Identify the good qualities, strengths, resources and positive intentions of each part in turn. Ask:

What does this part do for me?

What is its job in my life?

What are its special qualities?

What is its highest intention for me?

5) Ensure you arrive at a high intention for both parts. When you have arrived at the highest intention of one part for you, which will be a high value such as peace, love, joy, or contentment, **repeat step 4** for the other part.

6) Ask each part, in turn, if it recognizes the high value the other part has for you. Ask if the parts could work together for the good of the whole, now that they recognize they share the same or similar intentions. **Keep negotiating** until they agree. Get them to come to an agreement that they will both accept change. Get them to agree how this will work in the future.

7) Bring the hands together and scoop into the heart area. Hold them both there and allow the parts to integrate. Breathe, close your eyes and hold. When you are ready and feel the integration, allow the hands to release.

Allow yourself as much time as you feel you need for the integration and a full 3 minutes of quiet time after you complete the procedure.

You can certainly use this technique by yourself, but you may find that an experienced NLP Practitioner can get better results for you, at least the first time.

I have used it numerous times with clients and on myself with wonderful results.

For You To Do—Try One of These

Try out one of the exercises in this chapter for releasing negative emotions or beliefs, or changing a habit (EFT, Hypnosis, NLP).

Experiment with *Parts Integration* for conflicting emotions.

Tame a dragon! Play with it— make it your friend.

You will know when it has worked because you will feel a sense of release, like a burden dropping off your back or off your shoulders. It's a good feeling.

You will also know when it has worked because the issue disappears. Sometimes you can't remember what the problem was.

Remember, some of these techniques may need more than one attempt. If I have a really stubborn dragon I may use all of them to get rid of it. I tend to throw everything I can at a problem.

There are many different alternative techniques you can try which are beyond the scope of this book to explain. Here is a list of a few books that you may want to look into:

Time-line Therapy and the Basis of Personality by Tad James and Wyatt Woodsmall

The Emotion Code by Dr. Bradley Nelson

The Presence Process by Michael Brown

The Untethered Soul by Michael Singer

A New Earth by Eckhart Tolle.

Matrix Reimprinting by Karl Dawson.

Each of these books helped me a lot.

I especially love *Matrix Reimprinting* by Karl Dawson which is a technique he built onto EFT. In it Dawson goes back to the original imprint, or event, where the negative emotion or trauma was created. He then helps you, the client, change the story by imagining a different outcome, with different people or resources supporting the younger 'you' experiencing the event. Then you tap on the younger 'you' to get rid of the emotions and imagine a new picture that is more empowering.

There is not space here to go into detail of how to do this, but you can read the book or go on youtube to find explanations and demonstrations.

Time-Line Therapy also goes back to the original event and changes the memory. In the *Presence Process* Michael Brown outlines a simple way to reimprint new memories over traumatizing ones from the past. It is similar to reparenting the inner child.

I highly recommend trying out and experimenting with these methods of changing memories. They are highly effective and work quite quickly to effect lasting change.

Not everything works for everybody all the time. It's good to try out these different techniques and see what works for you. I can vouch that these processes certainly worked for me.

Now, let's continue the journey. We're going to confront the biggest dragon of all! And don't allow any sympathy for the devil…

Chapter 6

"Please Allow Me to Introduce Myself…": Beware the Saboteur!

"Late at night have you experienced a vision of the person you might become, the work you could accomplish, the realized being you were meant to be? Are you a writer who doesn't write, a painter who doesn't paint, an entrepreneur who never starts a venture? Then you know what Resistance is."

Stephen Pressfield—*The War of Art*

Let me introduce you to the most dangerous dragon of all—the *Saboteur*, sometimes known as Resistance. The *Saboteur* will undermine your best intentions and will resist all your efforts at self-improvement.

The moment you get inspired and determined to make a change the *Saboteur* is stimulated to act. It can be subtle and manipulative.

Some call it Resistance. Psychologists call it homeostasis. Freud called it the Death Wish. Religions (and the Rolling Stones) call it the Devil or Satan. It's our Inner Critic, that harsh internal judge that throws cold water on our ambitions. It seems to be a force that causes us to act against our own self-interest.

I'm guessing you are familiar with it.

It is the cause of people ruining their own success. It is the reason some millionaires go bankrupt as soon as they make their fortune. It is why some people, who have lost a lot of weight, suddenly gain it back. It's why reformed addicts, who have finally gotten their lives together, go on a binge and throw it all away. It's why lottery winners frequently lose all their winnings in a two week spending spree.

The *Saboteur* is responsible whenever someone does something inexplicable that seems to *sabotage* his or her best interests.

Resistance to Change

There is a part of your subconscious mind that is hardwired to resist change in order to protect you. This part dates back to primordial caveman times when early humans lived around a campfire. Safety lay within the circle of the fire and those who ventured outside risked death.

The circle of the fire was the *comfort zone*, which represented safety. Leaving the security of this circle could mean death from wild animals. Those who stayed close to the fire and took no risks remained safe.

Of course, some brave souls, the hunters, had to venture out to find food. But only the strongest and the fittest were chosen for this. They considered the risks carefully, went out armed, and returned quickly when their work was done.

For the rest of the group, staying close together around the fire assured the survival of the individual and the community. For continued survival, no unnecessary risks could be taken. Risks were frowned upon as threatening to the entire group.

A foolish individual who took unnecessary risks might be ostracized from the community; shunned. To be cast outside the circle was a death sentence. We are not designed to survive alone.

That's why we care what other people think.

As a human being your subconscious mind's primary objective is to protect you and keep you safe. Its natural tendency is to stop you from taking risks, dating back to caveman times.

Change = Risk = Threat

Any change in habits represents risk to your subconscious mind. Your subconscious is hardwired to stop you from making adjustments, even those that are rationally and logically good for you.

Our body has an inbuilt resistance to change as well. Homeostasis is an organism's natural tendency to maintain the status quo, to remain exactly as it is, in a condition of equilibrium or stability. If you ingest something poisonous, the whole body acts to neutralize it and get rid of it. If your blood becomes too acid your body will act quickly to restore the PH balance, even if it means sucking calcium from your bones.

Any change is registered immediately through a warning system: Danger! Change in the organism! Act promptly to redress normal balance!

This applies to individuals, families, social groups, tribes and nations as well. Notice how many groups are automatically resistant to innovation, especially political, religious, or educational organizations. The medical establishment will frequently resist implementing new policies that are obviously good for the patient, simply because they may be seen as a threat to the organization.

Homoeostasis is about survival; it holds things together, keeps them stable and maintains balance. It doesn't distinguish between changes for the better and changes for the worse; it resists all change.

Change equals risk equals threat, whether it's in the organism or in society.

So, for example, when someone stops smoking, even though it's good for the body, the body will resist the new development.

When someone starts to lose weight, even if the extra weight was harmful to health, there will be resistance from the organism. The metabolism will slow down to prevent any more weight loss because the weight loss is perceived as threat. *Warning! Starvation taking place! Take action to counteract!*

When someone tries to alter a habit, even if the habit is not serving him or her, the subconscious mind will resist the alteration. Always.

It will resist simply because it's different behavior. No other reason. The subconscious interprets it as equivalent to stepping out of the fire circle and into the dark night where wild animals lurk.

For the organism the status quo must always be maintained. This is why any transition is stressful to us, whether in our lifestyle, moving house, switching partners, starting a new gym regimen, or taking retirement. We find ourselves longing to return to the old ways and unwilling to settle into the new situation.

It is one of the reasons we cling to the past. This applies as well to you searching for your purpose and becoming a more authentic and realized person.

Any time we start on a new journey of the spirit we are likely to meet the *Saboteur*. Expect it. Be prepared for it.

Do not underestimate the power of this dragon! He is lurking there when you start your *Hero's Journey*. He would rather you stayed at home, surfing on the Internet or watching TV. He definitely prefers you on the sofa. He is waiting by the door to stop you going to the gym. *"Where are my keys?"* He is holding the refrigerator door open for you. *"I don't remember buying that ice cream. Can't waste it."* He will buy that pack of cigarettes and keep them handy. *"I need them around, just in case of emergency"* you hear yourself say.

The *Saboteur* has a pocketful of excuses at hand and is a master of delusion.

The Shadow Saboteur is Created

The *Saboteur* has its origins in this natural safety mechanism we are born with. It gets out of hand and becomes destructive as a result of our environment and upbringing.

Sometimes we are instilled with fear and discouraged from taking risks by people who care for us, in an effort to keep us safe. *"Watch out for strangers!" "Don't play near the water!" "Don't pet strange dogs, they might bite!"*

Parents, teachers, the opinions of our peers, and our experiences as we grow up form our beliefs about what is possible and impossible for us to achieve.

Combined with the inherent tendency to resist change, this can sometimes strangle our ambitions and our desires, and undermine our goals. And while it may be good advice not to pet strange dogs, if danger is emphasized too much, we become afraid to take any risks.

The Shadow *Saboteur* is created.

The *Saboteur* can be responsible for unexplained accidents, addictions, chronic illnesses and the *Victim* mentality.

He or she is the little voice whispering in your ear, "you're not good enough". "You will fail if you try that." "You'll make a fool of yourself and you will never succeed." "What will people think?"

Other people are always more clever, talented and skilled than you could ever hope to be. *"You can't do that! What were you thinking?"*

It may be the familiar voice of a parent or teacher, or that kid in school who used to make fun of you. Or it may be your own voice, chronically worrying about what other people think. *"Don't disapprove of me! Don't exclude me! I'll do what you want!"*

Be aware! This voice is subtle and clever. It will hide behind helplessness and low energy. It will hole up inside chronic illnesses. It will disguise itself behind circumstances and events in your life.

The Saboteur as Victim

The voice will play the Victim card with you: "It's not your fault, you can't help the way you are, you are not responsible. It's their fault."

The Victim will persuade you to blame everything but yourself for your problems. "My metabolism is out of whack, or maybe it's my thyroid. I hardly eat a thing. That's why I can't lose weight."

Or, (and I've heard myself say this) "I get low blood sugar when I diet. I nearly faint. I must have hypoglycemia." Seriously?

Or how about this one:

"I've always had poor health since I was very little. I had glandular fever, or was it rheumatic fever? Never been healthy since then. Nothing I can do about it."

Right. Nothing at all.

This voice will stop you writing that book, painting that picture, or starting that new business. It will certainly stop you heading towards the gym. *"Don't you have a cold coming on?"*

It will talk you out of taking any risks, and from living your dream. "Aren't you getting too old for this? Isn't it time you slowed down? Shouldn't you be acting your age? Go easy on yourself."

It will impede your progress and prevent you from finding your purpose in any way it can. It pretends to be your friend. *"I'm just trying to protect you."*

The Saboteur As Prostitute

The *Saboteur* becomes the *Prostitute* when we compromise our true heart's desires for comfort and survival. We do this sometimes without realizing it. We stay at the job we hate because we need the money. We marry the person we don't love in order to have financial security. We stay in a bad situation because we are afraid of what might happen if we move. *Better the devil you know...*

The *Prostitute* uses fear to manipulate you. It is operating in you whenever you sell out your dreams and hopes for money or security.

She will convince you that you can't take the risk, that it will never work, that you will fail and become destitute if you leave the security that she has sold you out to.

She usually shows up in the realms of relationships and work. Be aware! It is simply the *Saboteur* operating under another guise. It's just trying to keep you safe, in a misguided way.

Saboteur—Friend or Foe?

Some people, usually successful risk takers, don't seem to have a *Saboteur* at all. Donald Trump, Picasso, Margaret Thatcher, successful politicians, some movie stars and musicians, famous sportsmen and entrepreneurs seem totally impervious to what other people think of their chances of success. They succeed despite heavy opposition.

They go ahead and do their thing and let criticism roll off them like water off a duck's back. They become enormously, outrageously
successful because they have no internal voice telling them they can't do it.

They harbor no self-doubt and have total self-belief. They are unstoppable.

Yet in many such cases, that total lack of an internal critic, which enabled their success in their chosen realm, can be their undoing in other venues. They can appear to lack discernment, the voice of reason, the reality check.

Donald Trump was vilified in his brief run for president of the United States, in part because he just didn't seem to be able to hear how people were responding to his message. Tiger Woods had no internal critic telling him his behavior off the golf course was unacceptably risky. Margaret Thatcher was hounded out of office when she completely ignored popular outrage over the Poll Tax.

The very behaviors that made them successful in one arena ensured their demise in others. Their total self-belief was perceived as arrogance.

They seem to have **slain** their *Saboteur* when maybe they should have **tamed** it.

It seems the best bet is to make friends with our *Saboteur* and keep it around for when we need it. We *need* an internal reality check now and again. We benefit from discretion. We profit from having a voice telling us when we've gone too far. We do well to have some sensitivity to what other people are thinking.

We need to make the *Saboteur* our ally and not our undoing. We just need to make sure it doesn't get out of hand.

How Do We Befriend the Saboteur?

The best way to befriend the *Saboteur* is to become aware of when it is operating in you. **Self-awareness is the first step**. When you become of aware of it you can be prepared for it and pre-empt any negative influence.

So begin to notice how you sabotage your own success. When do you make excuses for your actions, your habits or your self-limiting beliefs?

Do you ever talk to yourself like this?

"I need to smoke, (eat cake, watch TV, take tranquilizers, have a drink), because it relaxes me."

"Nobody in my family knows how to make money – we're just not like that."

"I can't stand marketing or selling. It seems so unethical to me."

"I was just brought up that way. I can't change."

"I have all these health issues – I couldn't possibly attempt that."

"A little time on Facebook is a nice way to take a break."
(A favorite)

What are all these excuses trying to prevent you from becoming or doing?

—**Notice inexplicable accidents**. What was your subconscious trying to prevent you from doing?

—**Notice chronic complaints or illnesses.** What are they preventing you from achieving?

—**Notice** your **usual array of excuses** for not accomplishing things you'd like to accomplish.

What are the reasons you tell yourself you haven't achieved your goals?

What is the reason you tell yourself that you're overweight or unfit, not making enough money or that you never embarked on that career?

The *Saboteur* doesn't really mean to hurt us. But, like one of these robotic machines in science fiction movies, it relentlessly does what it has been programmed to do; keep us safe at all costs. That means preserving the status quo.

Negotiating With The Saboteur

The *Saboteur* needs to be convinced that a particular change is good for us if we want to make that change easily. We need to reassure it that the change is what *we* want and that it is in the best interests of the whole. The *Saboteur* will listen if we can convince it that unless we change we are at a much higher risk than if we do nothing.

Hypnosis is an enormously effective technique you can use to befriend the *Saboteur* and to facilitate negotiation.

When clients come to me to stop smoking, what I do is work with their *Saboteur* to convince it that giving up cigarettes is crucial for the health of the body. I present reasons why the change being proposed is a good thing and that the client must have the *Saboteur* on board to help.

I talk to the *Saboteur* while the client is in trance and convince it to actually assist the client in making the changes required to quit smoking. Without this buy-in, stopping smoking becomes a battle between the *Saboteur* and the conscious will to change. Guess who will always win?

Parts Integration can also be helpful in befriending the *Saboteur*. This technique, described in Chapter 4, involves a negotiation between the part that wants to change and the resisting part, the *Saboteur*. The parts are made to see that they have the same higher intention for the whole and can be persuaded to work together.

The *Saboteur* part is given a new role that doesn't undermine change but stays alert to danger. It maintains its discriminating abilities without becoming a nag, a critic, a harsh judge or a downer. It is no longer the cynical voice that throws cold water on new intentions.

The *Saboteur* becomes the watchdog, which keeps an eye on security but doesn't interfere with what its master is doing. It no longer bites the invited guest.

Everyone is happy. Change takes place and, given enough time to stick, eventually becomes the new status quo.

Two Ways To Instigate Change

There are two ways to approach making changes: **abruptly** or **gradually**.

Abrupt change is when we go cold turkey on an addiction. We stop smoking immediately and completely. We throw out our last pack of cigarettes and vow to never smoke again. We pour that bottle of wine down the drain.

Or, we may start a new diet—today. We throw out everything that contains sugar and carbohydrates: crackers, all processed food, cereals, bread, rice, pasta and sugary drinks. We start our new eating regime with determination and willpower.

Have you ever started a new exercise program? You sign up at the gym, or a 3 times a week Pilates or Yoga class. Or, you start weight training with a new instructor and begin jogging every morning.

These are examples of abrupt change. The *Saboteur* usually lies low the first few days when you are full of motivation and willpower. It lurks around until about day 3 or 4 of your exercise regime, when your muscles are aching and you're feeling tired. It whispers that "*it would really be better for you to stay in bed today ...just turn over and go back to sleep. That's right ...*"

You forget where you put your yoga mat just as you get ready to set off for that yoga class. Aw, it's too late to go now. Next time.

It usually waits until day 7 or 8 to show up when you stop smoking. This is about the time you are starting to think how easy it is. You're doing well. It whispers in your ear – *"this is so easy for you. One little cigarette won't hurt. You're so strong!"*

Of course, we know the results of listening to that voice.

If you decide abrupt change is the best way for you, hiring a coach to help you through those danger periods can be incredibly effective to counteract this happening. The coach will provide an alternative voice to the *Saboteur*, reminding you of what you want to achieve and warning you of what will happen if you backslide.

This is the way Alcoholics Anonymous operates—it keeps the danger of backsliding in your face at all times.

Regular self-hypnosis is also effective in reminding the *Saboteur* periodically to back off and get with the program.

The **slow approach to change** is when we taper off a bad habit rather than going cold turkey. Some smokers find this approach works best for them. They set goals for cutting back until eventually they are down to one cigarette a day, which they then easily give up.

The exercise regime is taken up slowly starting with one session a week and gradually working up to 3 or 4, giving you plenty of time for rest and recovery in the beginning.

You start the diet slowly, cutting out one or two targeted foods before going full force and cutting out all of them. It may include a day of eating your favorite foods without guilt, or indulging in your favorite dessert.

The advantage of the slow approach is that it can fool the *Saboteur* and it doesn't even show up to interfere. The change is so gradual you can bypass that resistance.

If you can manage to keep a new behavior going for at least 3 weeks, you can install it and it becomes the status quo.

The danger of the slow approach is that you possibly never fully commit to the complete change. You just tweak it at the edges.

You cut back on cigarettes but never move from 5 a day to zero. Or, you cut out rice, but never manage to get to sugar. Just one cookie won't hurt.

Here too a coach can help enormously to keep you on track. Many of my clients prefer the slow approach because it keeps the change under the radar. No alarm bells go off and it's easier. Having a coach ensures they stay on target and push through to achieve their ultimate goal.

Self-help and support groups can keep you on track for change. These are ways to bypass the *Saboteur* or keep it under control.

The Universe is Trying to Whack You on the Head with a Message

Another approach to the *Saboteur* is to consider that it is trying to give you a message from the Universe. When it interferes with your life it is showing that it is deeply unhappy about something you are doing. Treat it as a friend who is a little misguided at times but wants to help you.

It may feel there are lessons you need to learn.

Ask your subconscious mind what it is trying to tell you. Reassure it that you will take its concerns into account. Reassure it that when you make changes you will be careful. That's all it wants to know.

When we make friends with our subconscious mind, where the *Saboteur* lives, and learn how to communicate with it through awareness, meditation, hypnosis and the other techniques for change outlined in this book, our lives become easier. We become more successful, we can make changes effortlessly, and we become more purposeful and focused.

We stop tripping ourselves up when we are on the brink of success.

The *Saboteur* can be a powerful ally. With it on your side you can discover your purpose without interference and begin to age with passion and courage.

Slay That Dragon

We discussed taming and befriending dragons, but not slaying them. So which dragons would we want to slay, and why? We really need to slay those dragons that we have no use for whatsoever anymore. The lessons are learned, the story has been told many times and they are just holding us back.

These are the dragons that have arisen from abuse or violence or traumatic situations: dragons of self-loathing, feelings of worthlessness, extreme and unreasonable fear, excessive guilt from the past, shame, excessive grief from tragedy, overwhelming anger and resentment towards an abuser. There is no need to negotiate, befriend or compromise with these dragons; they need to go, now.

We also need to slay the dragons of life threatening addictions such as drugs, alcohol or other dangerous behaviors. Sometimes there is no time to negotiate and find the positive intention—just kill these off. They will kill you first if you don't act decisively. Get help. Now.

Usually in these instances, the story is old and has been repeated many times. It's time to kill it, once and for all. You may find professional help a great boon in these circumstances, so I highly recommend you find a trusted professional to talk to who specializes in addictions if these situations apply to you.

Deprogramming the Saboteur

When you notice yourself making excuses, **counter the excuses with affirmations.** In this way you can begin deleting the old programs and creating new, more empowering ones.

Emile Coue, the well-known French psychologist who lived in the first half of the 20th century, popularized the method of **autosuggestion,** which is similar to self-hypnosis. He is most famous for his mantra-like, conscious autosuggestion:

"Every day, in every way, I'm getting better and better."

You may have heard this before. Some people groan when they hear it, because it has become a cliche. But let me explain why this statement is so brilliant. It uses what is called "artfully vague" language—in other words, it is deliberately non-specific. This allows the subconscious mind to fill in the details and to supply whatever will work for you individually. Therefore, there is no resistance, because there is nothing to resist. I highly recommend you try it for yourself.

Here are some other statements you can use to counteract the negative programming that others have installed in you. Many therapists suggest using *"I am..."* followed by a positive statement. I recommend using *"I can..."* and I'll tell you why. When you first start countering the negative programming, you may find a lot of resistance from the *Saboteur.* If you say, *"I am wonderfully successful at what I do",* you may hear an internal voice saying, *"Oh yeah? Really?"* Instead, try *"I CAN be successful at my new project!"* Once again, there is nothing to resist. Anyone can.

Play with some of these and notice how they feel. Use statements that feel good, exciting, and possible. Avoid ones where you hear the negative voice. Some of my favorites:

"I CAN be wonderfully successful."

"I CAN achieve my perfect weight."

"I CAN be fit and healthy."

"I CAN get better and better with age!"

Find ones that work for you.
How about this:

"Every day, in every way, I'm feeling younger and younger!"

In some societies, getting older is seen as a positive thing. Think about it; there are many amazingly wonderful aspects to getting older. You are wiser, more experienced, more relaxed about yourself. You know how to wear your hair, after trying out many unsuccessful hairstyles; you know how to dress for your body, after experimenting with umpteen different fashions; you know what exercise works for you, after suffering hours in the gym or at that aerobics class. You just simply don't do things you don't like doing anymore. In so many ways, life is so much better with age!

Questions To Uncover Your Saboteur

When and how do you undermine your own success?

When do you blame something outside of yourself for your problems?

In what areas of your life have you compromised yourself for safety and security?

Do you suffer unexplained accidents? What are the circumstances? What do you think causes them?

In what areas of your life are you stuck, not making progress?

Limiting Beliefs

How much money do you believe you can make?

What level of fitness do you believe you can be and what weight you can achieve?

How successful can you can be?

What quality of relationship do you believe you can sustain with someone?

How disciplined in your habits?

Notice **inexplicable accidents**. What was your subconscious trying to prevent you from doing? What are you subconsciously gaining from this?

Notice **chronic complaints or illnesses**. What are they preventing you from achieving? What is the secondary gain?

Notice **your usual array of excuses** for not accomplishing things you'd like to accomplish.

Look at these questions and answer the ones that resonate with you. Don't agonize over any of them; they are there to stimulate your thinking. Now let's move on to a subject that is much more fun…

Chapter 7

"Well I Dreamed I Saw the Knights in Armor, Coming...": Archetypes — Mysterious Guides for Your Journey

"There's nothing you can do that's more important than being fulfilled. You become a sign, you become a signal, transparent to the transcendent; in this way, you will find, live, and become a realization of your own personal myth."

Joseph Campbell—*Pathways to Bliss*

Everybody loves a treasure hunt! You are about to embark on an exciting hunt for your Holy Grail, or, in other words, your purpose or meaning in life.

For this hunt you will need guides, mysterious beings who will help you on your way. They are just waiting for your instructions.

To find our treasures, our skills and abilities, we also need to connect with who we are: our True Self, Higher Self, or as some call it, our Authentic Self. And that *Old Hippie* living in the deepest recesses of your heart.

In this chapter I want to introduce you to Archetypes, explaining what they are and how you can discover yours. Working with Archetypes is a powerful way to help you understand who you are and why you do what you do. They are a secret key to becoming authentic.

Discovering my Archetypes has been incredibly enlightening, fun, and helpful in my own personal journey; learning how to work with them and uncovering their messages for me was life changing. This is an important step in finding your purpose and connecting with your passion. Please pay attention to this section. It holds a key to your success. I think you will enjoy it.

Discovering Your Archetypes

The term Archetype was first used by Carl Gustav Jung, the famous Swiss psychiatrist and psychotherapist, to signify ancient patterns of personality that appear in the world's myths, legends, and folk tales.

Archetypes are the characters you play in your life story. They are the essence of different personality types, the prototype, the pure energy of a particular style of character. They are embodiments of different aspects of the human psyche.

Archetypes are mythic examples of human beings, primordial personifications of character and temperament. Some well-known examples are the *King, Hero, Artist, Hunter, Rebel, Free Spirit, Rescuer, Seductress, Princess, Daddy's Little Princess, The Godfather, Seeker, Mystic, and Court Jester.* And don't forget *the Hippie.*

These are but a few examples of colorful personas that represent different natures operating in us, defining who we are. They make up our character and our uniqueness. They dictate our passions, interests and actions. We may be only vaguely aware of them until they are called to our attention.

We are born with our Archetypes and they define who we are.

Frequently, the moment we hear about them, their energies start to resonate within us and excite us. The unconscious mind thinks in the language of metaphor, of symbols and Archetypes. We intuitively understand this language.

Mythological characters that appear in legends and fairy tales are always Archetypes. A myth is an ancient tradition or story that has enduring meaning. It expresses universal themes that transcend time and culture and are fundamentally symbolic and allegorical.

Archetypes are the human expression of universal themes and are the pure embodiment of different types of human beings. They dance across the sky at night as the zodiacal *Hunter* and *Huntress*, they populate ancient Greek stories, they appear in fairy tales and legends, their faces are on Tarot cards and they are found in films and classic stories. We know them instinctively because they are part of us.

Jung says they are the shared heritage of the human race and dwell in the *Collective Unconscious*, i.e., the universal mind shared by all humanity.

My Inner Circle Of Archetypes

I discovered Archetypes when I was experiencing those major changes in my life that I discussed earlier, and was unsure what direction I wanted to take. I will never forget picking up the book called *Sacred Contracts* by Caroline Myss. I began reading about how Myss, a medical intuitive, became aware of Archetypes operating in her clients and how she saw these ancient characters rising up around them, trying to communicate with her.

It was then a light exploded in my brain and I suddenly saw *my* Archetypes and *my* whole life in a flash of insight.

I enthusiastically began studying Archetypes; I read about the *Seeker* Archetype; this Archetype passionately craves knowledge and spiritual truth and obsessively seeks it out from whatever source. Wow! That was a perfect description of me! I resonated and vibrated with familiarity. All my life I had been chasing from one spiritual path to the next, devouring books, workshops, lectures, and getting excited about different religions and new ideas.

I learned that each Archetype has two sides—a positive side and a shadow side. The shadow side of the *Seeker* is the *Lost Soul*, perpetually wandering in the wilderness, never able to settle with an idea or belief, always hoping the truth lies in the next book, guru or workshop.

That resonated with me too, unfortunately.

The *Seeker* then led me on to discover my *Warrior* (always looking for battles), the *Teacher* (always wanting to share knowledge), the *Pioneer* (always interested in new paths), the *Rebel* (ALWAYS getting into trouble and pushing back against accepted norms), and the *Magician/Shaman* (fascinated with transformation and the esoteric). These were all familiar friends, guides, and companions in life.

The *Hippie* is an offshoot of the *Rebel*. I also have a *Gnostic* in me, which is also related to the *Rebel* and the *Mystic*.

These Archetypes defined who I was and explained why I acted the way I did. They were my guides and soul mates.

I began working with them to help find my path and to figure out what I was meant to be doing with my life. I learned that each Archetype has a reason to be in your life, a contract you need to honor. Each has a lesson to teach that helps you find your path and true purpose.

As you begin to understand yourself better you have a better chance of living a fulfilling and exciting life, and of finding your niche.

Who Are Your Archetypes?

How do you discover your own personal Archetypes? You discover them by answering questions about yourself—about your interests, skills, and personality traits. (See the list of questions at the end of this chapter)

For example my mother always used to say I came out mad when I was born and have been fighting ever since. My *Rebel* and *Warrior!*

I have always been interested in spiritual ideas, religions and ideologies. I took my first degree in Theology and Comparative Religion. This is the *Seeker*—always searching for wisdom and truth from any source, and excited by new ideas.

I love reading and researching, and then sharing what I have learned. *Teacher*.

My family would say I have always been stubborn and determined to do things my way. *Rebel* again!

I left Alabama at 18 and have only gone back to visit. I have lived in foreign countries most of my adult life. *Pioneer, Seeker, Adventuress.*

One of my best skills is public speaking. *Teacher* again, with a little *Actress* in there.

Do you get the idea? What you love and your personal characteristics give clues to your Archetypes. These will be your most obvious ones. You may also have hidden or repressed ones. These are desires or inclinations that you have suppressed because they weren't convenient or you were taught they were wrong for you.

Repressed Archetypes can make us unhappy and frustrated! With the exercises in this chapter you can find yours. Do you have a repressed *Artist*? This is common. People are frequently not encouraged to go into art because of the dire financial implications. Your *Artist* may be languishing. A repressed *Old Hippie*?

My *Warrior* went AWOL (absent without leave) at one point in my life and I started to live someone else's story. I had to bring him back to live life on my terms again.

An Art, Not a Science

It's important to know that finding your Archetypes is an art, not a science. There are no consequences for getting it wrong. There is no wrong. Whatever comes to you is right.

Your Archetypes can be either gender and they don't need to correspond to your gender. I have several male Archetypes.

Use the list of Archetypes included at the end of the book to stir your imagination. You may want to choose a name for an Archetype that isn't listed. There are basic Archetypes and many variations on those Archetypes. The list is a mix of basic Archetypes, shadow Archetypes and common variations of the basic ones.

For instance, the *Advocate* can be known as the *Activist, Attorney, Champion, Crusader, Defender,* or *Environmentalist.* My *Business Woman* is an off–shoot of my *Warrior*—that part of me that engages actively with the world and is competitive and savvy. The *Artist* can be called the *Writer, Actor, Sculptor* or *Musician* for example.

Choose the name of an Archetype that suits you and has the flavor you like. One of my clients, who seemed to have a *Wanderer* Archetype, balked at this until she discovered the alternative name of *Free Spirit*, which is the same Archetype with a

97

different name. She loved that name and it resonated with her and made her feel happy.

You will usually find that when you discover one of your Archetypes you feel happy and content with it. We tend to be quite proud of our Archetypes. I once told a friend she had a *Witch* Archetype, wondering what her response would be. She broke into a huge grin. *"Yes,"* she said, *"Exactly! That's me!"*

We tend to think everyone has the Archetypes we have. Not true. My sister has a *Cheerleader* Archetype. She is loyal to her tribe, the team—supportive and positive at all times. She is also very conventional and plays by the rules. She loves family, country, church. She doesn't like for people to rock the boat. The *Cheerleader* is the exact opposite of the *Rebel*. Family members don't always share Archetypes!

It's also important to remember that Archetypes are essentially neutral. There are a few Archetypes that seem to be malevolent, but what you are seeing is the shadow side of a neutral Archetype. Each Archetype has a good side and bad side—the shadow side— and a lesson for you in this life. Sometimes the shadow is better known than its more benign side, such as the *Addict* and the *Prostitute*.

If the shadow side dominates it is the consequence of that Archetype going to the extreme; unbridled and unchecked. The *King* can become a *Tyrant*. The *Queen* can become a *Drama Queen*. The *Student* can become the *Eternal Student*. The *Flirt* can become a *Black Widow*. The *Nomad* or *Free Spirit* can become the *Beggar*. The *Advocate* can become the *Eco-terrorist*.

So, are you a Queen, a King, Princess, Shaman, Hero, Warrior, an Artist, Musician, Rescuer, Caretaker, Guru, Healer, Trickster, Court Jester, Godfather, Seductress, Scholar, Teacher, Seeker or Nomad? Perhaps you are an Engineer, Scientist, Advocate or Domestic Goddess?

Your Archetypes can sometimes appear to contradict each other. That's fine. You may have a *Virgin* and a *Seductress* at the same time. You could have a *Priest* or *Holy Man* as well as a *Hedonist*. That's what makes you so interesting and complex.

Archetypes In Public Life

We see Archetypes everywhere in public life. Politicians embody different Archetypes, sometimes unwittingly.

Mitt Romney lost the last presidential election in the United States, in part because he unknowingly embodied the *Shape-shifter* Archetype. This is an Archetype that can enable you to change appearances and personas to adapt to the situation.

As Caroline Myss points out, this Archetype has a shadow aspect, which is unstable, fickle, and lacks conviction. It reinvents itself to appeal to whatever is the latest trend. Romney revealed this Archetype on a number of occasions and it didn't help him. Nobody wanted a President who seemed to keep changing his stance to please others.

Those politicians who embody the *Statesman* or *Leader* will most likely win presidential elections. Archetypes are extremely important in public life.

On the positive side, the *Shape-shifter* is a great Archetype for an actor. Some actors are able to identity with and personify totally different characters with each film they act in. Others prefer to play the same character every time. Either choice can bring success. John Wayne embodied his Archetype—the *Hard-bitten Hero*—and played him to great success in every film.

A *Shape-shifter* can also work well behind the scenes in politics, in negotiator roles, marketing, or as an ambassador. Eli Gold, the character in the TV series The Good Wife (another Archetype), who played the part of campaign manager, was a classic *Shape-shifter*.

We don't like it when archetypal actors play against type. Paul Newman played a scoundrel in one film and it flopped. Paul was the archetypal *Good Guy*.

In the age of social networking it's harder and harder for public figures to fake an Archetype. If you try to take on a persona that is not one of your true Archetypes it will eventually show. We have numerous examples of this phenomenon: televangelists who sleep with members of their flock, politicians who preach about ethics and dip their hands in the till, sportsmen who pretend to be good family men, who aren't.

You see many celebrities today jumping on the charity bandwagon. You can always tell which ones are genuine and have the relevant Archetype, and which ones are hoping for good publicity. The mask will eventually slip and all is revealed, sometimes resulting in great scandal and downfall.

Organizations and Archetypes

Almost every group will have an Archetype it embodies. It's fun to notice and figure out which ones are operating. If you join a group and find you just don't fit in, it may be because you don't resonate with the group Archetype. This applies to churches, religions, companies.

Different organizations and movements will take on an Archetype persona. The gay community embraces the *Queen (Drama Queen)* with humor. Alcoholics Anonymous takes on the *Victim* (you have an illness, it's not your fault), as well as the *Addict* (you will be an alcoholic the rest of your life).

Some question the wisdom of insisting someone will always have an addiction and of forcing the person to identity with that addiction. Nevertheless, AA is undoubtedly successful in helping people. It forces them out of denial and provides a stable structure for them to plug into. It keeps the *Saboteur* at bay.

100

Firemen embrace the *Hero, the Rescuer*, and the *Knight in Shining Armor*. Many people fantasize about being rescued by one of these attractive Archetypes. They are irresistible at a deeply unconscious (archetypal) level!

Be wary of self-help groups that anchor members in the shadow *Victim* syndrome, blaming others for their problems, encouraging self-pity and touchiness around their issues, and making the abuse or problem their identity. Members may hold onto their problems as a way to retain approval and membership in the group. We like to be part of a tribe.

Many support groups do an enormous amount of good and provide much needed assistance for people in distress. The key is to know which Archetype the group is embracing and when it's time to leave and get on with life. To recognize the *Innocent Child* is very different from taking on the *Eternal Victim*.

The most successful groups embrace the *Warrior*, the Archetype that can help members enforce their boundaries and win their battles. A strong *Warrior* is crucial for self-esteem and enables us to take responsibility for our lives.

Questions To Discover Your Archetypes

What have you always been interested in?

What do older members of your family say you've always been like? (E.g. She's always been rebellious. He's always loved anything mechanical. You can't keep her away from X. He's always loved X.)

What personality characteristics have you always had?

How would a good friend describe you?

What subjects interested you in school or college?

Ideally what would you spend your spare time doing?

Answer these questions as best you can. Each answer will give a clue to an Archetype.

Choose a few (up to 12) Archetypes that seem to fit you and express who you are. Use the list in the appendix to spur your imagination.

Good work! Now let's go explore how to work with your Archetypes and find their messages for you.

Chapter 8

"There's a Star-man Waiting in the Sky...": How Your Archetypes Can Help You

"Archetypal patterns awaken in us our own divine potential. They can liberate us from the limitations of our thoughts and feelings. They can help us shed light on the dark or little–known corners of our souls and amplify our own brilliance and strengths."

Caroline Myss—*Sacred Contracts*

Discovering which Archetypes you embody and working with them is one of the quickest paths to finding your role in life. They can help you determine what you should be doing right now and are the keys to connecting to your True Self.

Archetypes are guides; they are eager to communicate with you and to give you advice and wisdom, but you first need to open up to their energies.

To make sure you get the most out of this chapter, first go through the list in the appendix and choose up to 12 Archetypes that resonate with you, and that reflect your interests and personality. Have fun with this. There is no right or wrong. Just follow what feels correct.

You have primary and secondary Archetypes. The secondary ones are those that you have a tendency for but they are not dominant.

Now choose one that seems to really be your major Archetype, the one that is really the essence of you.

Mine is the *Seeker*. The *Seeker* is always searching for spiritual truth, for the answers to life's big questions. The *Seeker* is interested in wisdom wherever it may be found and loves to follow new paths, explore new religions, read new books and study wisdom literature. The *Seeker* has influenced almost every major decision in my life and is the driving force behind many of my activities and life choices.

Communicating With Your Archetype

Now go somewhere quiet with a notebook and pen and take a few minutes to reflect on this Archetype that most closely represents you. Caroline Myss calls it having an "interview" with your Archetype.

1) **Imagine the Archetype** standing in front of you. What does it look like? How is it dressed? What gender is it? Invoke this Archetype to come to you. Call it by name.

Frequently people report they imagine their Archetypes look sort of medieval, like personas on Tarot cards or like something out of a fairy tale or the zodiac. They have a timeless look to them—a "once upon a time" appearance.

2) **Now silently reflect on that Archetype** and how you know that Archetype is part of you.

"Why did I choose you? How is it that you resonate with me?"

"How have you operated in my life? How far back can I remember you being there? How have you influenced the course of my life? Relationships? Work and career? Finances?"

"How has your shadow side been operating in me?" (The shadow is the negative side of the Archetype)

3) **Now silently ask what its purpose is for you.**

"What life lessons do you have for me?"

"Do you have a message for me? Any advice? Can you guide me to my purpose?"

4) **Thank it and close the session.**

Do this exercise with as many Archetypes as you feel are yours. It's probably best to spread the interviews out over several days. Find the essence of what each one has to offer you and its message for you. Archetypes are guides that reside in your subconscious. They love to communicate and do so easily.

They will give you advice and guidance. They are especially good at helping with any creative activities.

Become aware of your Archetypes operating in your life. Notice how they affect your behavior and your choices.

Archetypes, Shadows, and Contracts

Each Archetype has a life lesson for you, a challenge and a purpose for being part of you. You can think of this as a *contract* that you need to honor. Understanding what the contract is about will help you understand your life purpose.

Remember each Archetype has a shadow side. The shadow appears when an Archetype goes to the extreme and its behavior is unchecked. The *Lover* becomes the *Vampire*. The *Warrior/Soldier* becomes the *Gun-for–Hire*.

The shadow is where you will find the contract embedded. The shadow side represents the special life challenges this Archetype brings to you. Look at the shadow and find your contract.

Take your list of Archetypes and beside each one write a statement that describes what you think its contract with you is about.

Here are some examples of contracts with my Archetypes. They represent challenges I have faced all my life:

Seeker—to find faith, certainty

Warrior—to choose my battles wisely when I engage in the world. To face my challenges courageously

Rebel—to learn what to trust, and what to accept. To avoid being overly cynical

Teacher—to live what I teach, to walk my talk

Magician/Shaman/Healer—to heal myself first and then others

Eternal Student—to gain expertise, to really understand something

Pioneer—to learn how to settle and be content

Old Hippie—to live authentically and not automatically accept everything I'm taught.

Archetypes and Relationships

Archetypes can help enormously in getting relationships to work. When you become aware of your own Archetypes you will understand yourself better. And the great thing is, you will start recognizing Archetypes in your friends and family and especially your significant other. By using this information you can get your relationships to run smoothly.

When I was first with my Mexican husband, before we were married, we argued a lot. I thought it was inevitable due to a clash of cultures: *Strong-Willed, Liberated, American Female meets Alpha, Latino, Supremely Self-Confident Male.*

Whoa. The sparks flew and we upset each other a lot. I really felt that the relationship was doomed if we couldn't find a way to get along more peacefully.

Then I discovered Archetypes and I promise you, we were married within 6 months. We've been happily married for 6 years now, and going strong. We hardly ever fight—well, maybe a spat here and there. I honestly can say that I owe it to understanding our Archetypes.

What did I learn that made such a difference? First I discovered that I had the Seeker, the Rebel, the Princess, the Warrior, the Teacher/Coach/Mentor, the Flirt/Seductress (now retired), the Eternal Student, and the Pioneer, among others.

He was a Yogi, Holy Man, Missionary, Midas, Innocent, Shaman, Preacher, and Businessman. The main clashes were coming when my Seeker and Eternal Student met up against his Missionary and Yogi Archetypes.

The *Missionary* knows what he believes, doesn't harbor doubts and is more than happy to tell you his point of view. He's on a mission to share his beliefs and change the world.

The *Seeker*, on the other hand, is never really sure of anything, always doubting what is being propounded and always willing to look at things from another angle.

The *Missionary* knows what he believes, doesn't harbor doubts and is more than happy to tell you his point of view. He's on a mission to share his beliefs and change the world.

The *Seeker*, on the other hand, is never really sure of anything, always doubting what is being propounded and always willing to look at things from another angle.

The Missionary in him could never understand why I needed to keep looking for the truth. He would frequently say to me, "Just find something you believe in and stick with it. Why do you need to read another book on that subject? You have the truth in this one." The truth he follows is yoga and meditation. He doesn't feel he needs to look further.

Finding "the truth"—the Holy Grail—is the elusive goal of the *Seeker*. It's easier said than done! For the *Seeker* you can't force belief, you can't "just decide" to believe something. The *Seeker* is always second-guessing and looking over his shoulder for the next big idea. When is the next workshop? Ooh, in Santa Fe did you say?

I also had the *Eternal Student*—similar to the *Seeker* but differing in many ways. The *Student* always wants to learn more and is always curious about new ideas, craving moments of insight. Reading books, studying new subjects, taking new courses and always chasing some sort of education are the *Student's* passionate pursuits. The *Eternal Student* doesn't necessarily care about putting knowledge into practice but just simply loves learning for the sake of learning.

The *Yogi* is about 'experiencing' knowledge and the truth. Words, beliefs and ideas are not what matter to the *Yogi*; experience and the results of experience are all that counts. *Yogis* were the original *Gnostics*. A *Yogi* is disciplined and self-controlled.

Can you see the potential for misunderstanding here? Although my husband wasn't against books and knowledge—he is very well educated—he grew frustrated with my becoming intoxicated with new ideas without bothering to put them into practice. In addition, my free-spirited *Rebel* contrasted with his disciplined *Yogi* life style.

Once I saw this clearly, I could see his point of view and was able to avoid conflict. It became so easy to be compatible. I was able to laugh at our differences. I relaxed and just let him do his thing and be who he was, and I did my thing. He is a lot more disciplined than I, and I had a lot to learn from that. Instead of arguing, I was able to let go, enjoy and even rely on his certainty about things.

Another clash was his *Innocent* and my *Flirt/Seductress*. She terrified him in the beginning and he didn't trust that aspect of me. I had a kind of flirty manner, quite American, which I used with many people. I was light-hearted, a little loud, confident and sometimes overly friendly with people I didn't know. He saw this as an invitation to be taken advantage of in his country, Mexico, where we live.

This openness didn't always translate well in a foreign culture. It worried him and he was concerned for my safety. At first, I saw this as an attempt to suppress me. However, when I realized what was going on—a clash of Archetypes as well as a clash of cultures—I toned my *Flirt* down and was able to see his side of things.

Besides, I didn't need her any more. She had done her job. Retirement time.

Notice, I worked on my point of view and didn't try to change his. It's not advisable to try to change other people; better to work on yourself instead. And do not mess with someone else's Archetype!

I learned from this the valuable lesson that you don't have to compromise who you are to get along with people. You can just adjust certain things and let others go that aren't important. Choose your battles wisely and just let people be who they are.

You may be thinking that two people with opposing Archetypes are not a good match, but the truth is, opposites can complement each other. It certainly is working well for us and we now bring out the best in each other. I have become more disciplined and a little more grown up while he has lightened up and become more accepting of free spirited, rebellious, pioneering, skeptical types. He married an *Old Hippie* after all.

Your Stage Of Life

"You must learn to know what is the Archetype of your stage of life and live it. Trying to live the Archetype of the stage that you have left behind is one of the basic causes of neurotic troubles."

Joseph Campbell—Pathways to Bliss

At different stages in our lives, we need different Archetypes operating in us. When you have honored your contract with an Archetype there may be no more need for it to continue operating in your life. You can retire it to the background. It will never fully disappear because it is part of your basic character, but you may want new ones to step in and assist you for new challenges you are facing.

Which Archetypes do you need to retire and which do you need to bring in? At one point in my life I needed to retire my *Princess*. She had a strong tendency to be a *Lazy Princess*. I needed to bring in a *Queen* who was ready to take responsibility for my life. I needed to grow up.

110

I also needed to bring in an Archetype that had discipline and perseverance to counter some of my habits and to help me with my career. I call this my *Business Woman*—no nonsense, hard working and motivated. She's the one who showed up when I was doing business training—competitive and no nonsense. She can face challenges. She will disappear quite easily if I'm not careful. She gets annoyed with me if the *Lazy Princess* raises her head or if she feels I'm not being serious enough. The *Business Woman* is an offshoot of the *Warrior*, that aspect of us that engages with the world.

I must emphasize that Archetypes do not disappear completely when we retire them or bring another more empowering one to the fore. They can come back unexpectedly or be brought in from pasture if we need them.

Hence the name of this book, *A Self-help Guide for the Old Hippie at Heart*. If you have that archetype, it will still be living deep within your heart and may be wanting to express itself.

How Do You Bring An Archetype Into Your Life?

First you need to identify which Archetype you need. Write down the qualities of that Archetype and imagine you are inviting it into your being. Ponder it, focus on it and ask it to come into your life.

You will need to make a new contract with this Archetype and you will need a plan for bringing it into your life. Visualize how your life will look when this Archetype is operating in your life. How will you feel? What will be happening? What will you be doing? Who will you be with?

What needs to change in your life to reflect your new Archetype?

How will you make these changes? What habits need to change?

MARGARET NASH

Some people enjoy pasting pictures around their home that represent the new Archetype. Write down the qualities you are missing and that you want brought in. Affirm to yourself, "*I allow this Archetype to be part of me now. I welcome in the qualities of X, X, and X.*"

One note of caution; it's important to bring an Archetype in that resonates with you and that is probably already part of you. For example, I could not bring in a *Scientist*—he just wouldn't come because there would be nothing in me for him to relate to, and I wouldn't be able to commit to him. I've tried to bring in the *Domestic Goddess* with the idea that I would then love to clean my kitchen. It didn't work. She would come now and then to cook a meal and then disappear. There has to already be a connection to the Archetype that you want to bring into your life.

My coach suggested that the word *Domestic* is why I can't bring that Archetype in. Domestic brings up resistance from the *Rebel* immediately. He suggested *Rebel Chef* might work better. She might not run off so quickly.

My contract with my *Business Woman* is that I will make the effort needed to succeed. I will work on my habits and my motivation. I have to commit that I will take her seriously. She won't be messed with. I like her. She's edgy and a bit bossy.

Bringing a new Archetype into your life requires action and a genuine commitment to change.

Honoring Your Contracts

Your contracts with your Archetypes need to be honored and fulfilled. If a contract is not honored an Archetype can go to the shadow side and you can become repressed and frustrated.

One of the most common examples of this is the *Artist*. There are many frustrated artists who do not honor their art. This is

112

usually because it's difficult to make a living with art and many young people are encouraged early in life to pursue other venues.

I have an *Advocate* Archetype. It's one of my secondary Archetypes. The *Advocate* in me has a strong sense of justice and gets very upset over injustices. I am always on the side of the underdog, championing oppressed people, underprivileged people, suffering factory farm animals, gays or women.

I would love to have been a lawyer of some sort, helping the underprivileged and fighting for justice. However, I was never encouraged to go into law because back in my day young southern ladies were encouraged to be librarians and teachers. But that's just my excuse. It would have required another 5 years of higher education and expense, and by the time I graduated from college I was ready to get on with other things. You see, it was a secondary Archetype.

I have not honored my contract with the *Advocate* Archetype. My advocacy these days consists of sounding off on social media from time to time and giving money to various activist organizations. My problem is that my *Advocate* Archetype has gone over to the shadow side, the *Bleeding Heart*. I am just too soft hearted and compassionate; injustices and suffering really upset me. A picture of a suffering person or animal can haunt me for ages.

A good *Advocate* needs to be tough, thick skinned, and objective to really serve a cause properly. The challenge this Archetype brings me, my contract, is to develop a more detached attitude.

What Archetypes do you need to acknowledge and honor?

Archetypes and Your Story

Archetypes play a major part in helping you define your role in life, discover your niche, and rewrite your script.

If you are living the roles of Archetypes that aren't really yours, you will feel unfulfilled, frustrated and out of sync with life. A common example of this is a woman forced to play *Domestic Goddess* or *Mother* when she doesn't have those Archetypes. You can still be a good parent without the *Mother* or *Father* Archetype, but you may chafe or get bored with some of the stuff that goes with it.

Not all women can be satisfied playing traditional female roles. Not all men can play masculine roles and be happy. The Baby Boomers are the first generation to persistently fight the stereotypes of male and female roles and recognize that when we force people to behave against type, we cause unhappiness.

Hippies really fought against roles that society had in mind for us. That's what we are fighting against now—the stereotypes for growing older.

It's so important that we discover our true Archetypes and distinguish them from roles imposed on us by society, parents, and expectations of others. It's a liberating experience and enables us to become aligned, focused and authentic.

Honoring our Archetypes is *crucial* for living passionately.

Are there any Archetypes you are not honoring? Can you discover them and figure out how to make them more active in your life? Is there something you've always wanted to do or be that you haven't pursued? Now may be the time to do it! What better time is there?

So if you have a repressed *Artist*—go sign up for that art class!

If you have a repressed *Advocate*—go get involved in a cause you support!

If you have a repressed *Warrior*—go out into the world and face those challenges you've been avoiding! Or, go into that cave and fight that dragon.

If you have a repressed *Old Hippie*—start rebelling against those stereotypes the world is pushing on you. Live the way you want to!

If Archetypes remain repressed they can cause dissatisfaction and vague feelings of frustration. The best way to honor a dormant Archetype *and* to bring a new one into your life is to take action.

114

Uncovering a repressed Archetype can lead you to new roles, a new sense of purpose, new, satisfying activities and your passion for life. Sometimes you can be very surprised by what you discover. My coach uncovered my languishing *Writer* Archetype sleeping in the corner of my office and prodded it into action.

Other people are frequently better than you are at discovering your hidden Archetypes.

By the same token, are you trying to live the role of an Archetype you just don't have? This can happen when an Archetype is imposed on you by parents and society. What were the expectations of you when you were growing up? Do they fit you? Are you trying to force yourself into roles that don't suit you and your talents?

A typical example would be a young man pushed into accounting by his parents when he really wanted to be a musician.

Have you been living an imposed role in life? Which one? Is it time to let it go? What Archetype will you replace it with?

Council Meetings

What I'm going to share with you next is the most effective way I know for tapping into the universal mind or "Collective Unconscious". Through this method you can get answers to burning questions, solve problems and find your purpose.

It is an amazing way to harness your Archetypes and allow them to help you.

It's like consulting the Oracle.

I call it my Council Meetings.

It's nothing new. Shamans call this kind of meeting a Fireside. When you take a shamanic journey to find your True Self you may meet with an imaginary Council of Elders around a fireside, whose members give advice and counsel.

Napoleon Hill in his seminal book, *Think and Grow Rich,*
describes meeting with his "Invisible Counselors":

"The procedure was this. Just before going to sleep at night, I
would shut my eyes, and see, in my imagination, this group of men
seated with me around my council table. Here I had not only an
opportunity to sit among those whom I considered to be great, but I
actually dominated the group, by serving as the chairman."

Hill met with his counselors, who were famous and successful
men from the past, (archetypes), on a daily basis for many years
and received untold wisdom and advice from them.

He says that as well as dispensing advice, many times they
helped him in difficult circumstances.

"On scores of occasions, when I have faced emergencies, some
of them so grave that my life was in jeopardy, I have been guided
miraculously past these difficulties through the influence of my
'Invisible Counselors'."

How My Meetings Came About

My first Council Meeting with my Archetypes came to me in
meditation one day, unannounced and unsolicited. Suddenly
appearing before me, in my mind's eye, was a large, oblong oak
table; I was at one end and my "Higher Self" at the other. One by
one personas came into the room and seated themselves around the
table. They identified themselves as my various Archetypes.

I asked a question that had been on my mind and the answers
started coming thick and fast. The advice was breathtakingly good
and I can attest that when I put it into action it worked perfectly.

After the first meeting I found that I could call them into
Council deliberately, like Hill did, whenever I needed help.
However, it only worked if I had a clear question that I wanted
advice on or if I needed help with creative ideas. If I was muddled,

I got nothing. Sometimes, if my mind wandered or if my question wasn't clear, the figures would just disappear, as if in rebuke. But, when everything was aligned it was brilliant.

How to Have Your Own Meetings

You can call your own Council Meetings. When you do, keep a notebook handy. Recording it immediately will ensure you remember what your guides say.

You can choose to use Hill's method and invite in heroic figures from history, or people you admire and want to learn from, alive or dead. These are Archetypes. Or, you can just ask if any of your Archetypes wants to join you and has a message for you. See what happens.

Hold the meeting for as long as you are getting information or ideas. Close it and thank them for communicating with you. It's always good to show gratitude for help and advice.

For those of you who are skeptical of guides or hazy beings from another dimension, think of this as a way to stimulate your own inner wisdom or unconscious mind. This can give you access to information hidden inside your own mind.

Artists, musicians and writers have been doing this throughout the ages, calling on their muses.

I think the results will astonish you, just as they did Napoleon Hill.

Working With Your Archetypes

1) Once you have identified your Archetypes, follow this **interview** procedure.

   *a) **Imagine the Archetype** standing in front of you. What does it look like, how is it dressed, what gender is it? Invoke this Archetype to come to you. Call it by name.*

b) *Now silently reflect how you know that Archetype is part of you. Why did you choose it? Why did it resonate with you?*

c) **Ask it these questions:** *"How have you operated in my life? How far back can I remember you being there? How have you influenced the course of my life? Relationships? Work and career? Finances?"*

d) **Do you see the shadow operating in you?** *How? (The shadow is the Archetype acting so extremely it becomes negative)*

e) *Now silently ask what* **its purpose is for you.** *"What lessons do you have for me? What do I need to learn from you?" "What is my contract with you?"*

f) **Ask what message it has** *for you. "Do you have a special message for me? Any advice for my life? Can you guide me to my purpose?*

g) *What is the* **special challenge** *it brings you in your life?*

h) **Thank** *it and close the session. Immediately record the answers.*

2) **Identify any Archetypes you may have repressed.**

"Do I have any repressed Archetypes? How can I honor them?"

"What have I always wanted to do, or had a special talent for, that I'm not doing?"

3) **Identify any Archetypes that you want to bring into your life.**

> *"What Archetypes can help me find my passion?"*
>
> *"Which Archetypes will help me fulfill my purpose?"*
>
> *"What Archetypes do I need to bring into my life?"*
>
> *"What Archetypes do I need to let go of? What roles have been forced on me by society that don't sit well with me?"*

4) Now you are ready for a **Council Meeting**.

After you have identified your Archetypes and interviewed several of them, sit in a quiet place and decide what question you want answered or advice you would like to receive.

Close your eyes and state your question. Announce you are calling a meeting.

Imagine you are sitting at a long table, or around a fireside, or in the audience of a theatre looking at the stage.

Visualize your Higher Self at the other end of the table or somewhere nearby.

State your question. Sit quietly and invite your Archetypes, or whatever guides have relevant information for you, to come in.

Keep asking the question until you start getting answers. Allow the answers to come of their own accord. Do not force them.

Close the meeting and thank them for their guidance.

119

Now you have explored who you really are and becoming more aware of your authentic self. Let's keep moving. In the next chapter we will discover how to find your true heart's desire!

Chapter 9

"We are Stardust, We are Golden...": Finding Your True Heart's Desire

"You grow old when you lose interest in life, when you cease to dream, to hunger after new truths and to search for new worlds to conquer. When your mind is open to new ideas, new interests, and when you raise the curtain and let in the sunshine and inspiration of new truths of life and the universe, you will be young and vital."

Joseph Murphy—*The Power of Your Subconscious Mind*

Let's recap how you got to this point in the journey.

The **challenge**: You may have lost your juice for life and have no strategy for stepping into the next stage of life. You are missing your burning desire, your motivation. You don't know what your role is anymore and you don't know what you want in life.

The **trigger**: This may have come on slowly with the realization that you are getting older, or it may have been precipitated by an outside crisis in your life, such as divorce, kids leaving home, financial difficulties or retirement. Something has left you feeling like you are living in the wrong story.

Acknowledge: You have discovered how important it is to acknowledge the situation you are in—transition shock— and to accept that help is needed. You need to relax and cocoon.

Consequences: You feel life is slipping away and you are spinning your wheels. You feel like if you don't find your purpose soon, it may be too late.

Solution: To set off on your *Hero's Journey* to find your True Self, your True Heart's desire and to rewrite your story for living

Step 1: The first step is letting go of what is over in your life. It may involve a grieving process—for your old job, your old relationship, or your old identity. Someone close to you may have died. Whatever the circumstances, you need to grieve and let go before you can move on and find your way out of the forest.

Step 2: You have set off to confront your dragons of Resistance—negative emotions, limiting beliefs, and bad habits/addictions or old ways of doing things. You have faced the biggest dragon of all, the *Saboteur*, who will try to stop you from making any changes in your life.

Step 3: You are discovering your Archetypes—primordial, ancient personas who have always been part of you and who define your character and personality. These are your guides who will help you find your purpose.

Step 4: Now, it is time for you to find your passion, your purpose, your "true heart's desire" and to rewrite your script for living that works for you right now.

Finding Your Purpose, Your Unused Potential

"Whatever your age, your upbringing, or your education, what you are made of is mostly unused potential. It is your evolutionary destiny to use what is unused, to learn and keep on learning for as long as you live. To choose this destiny, to walk the path of mastery, isn't always easy, but it is the ultimate human adventure."

George Leonard—Mastery

Let's talk about purpose. Why is it so important to find your purpose? Do we have one purpose or can we have many in our lives? Does your purpose change with time?

How does finding your purpose help you to age rebelliously?

This is how. Being in touch with our purpose is what gives us motivation and interest in life. It makes us excited to wake up in the morning and to get on with our day. Our time becomes full of useful activity and we deeply enjoy ourselves.

When we have a sense of purpose we know what we want to be doing with our time. All our activities align and we become unstoppable.

When we find our purpose we tap into our unused potential and pursue the ultimate human adventure. We no longer worry about getting older—we're too busy with more important things. If we are living *without* a sense of purpose we can feel stuck and lack energy or enthusiasm. Chronic fatigue or illness sometimes sets in. We feel our age.

However, the idea of searching for their purpose is a pretty daunting proposition for many people. It can feel overwhelming to try and find *the* one purpose that we are living for. What if we come up with the wrong one? Can we get it wrong?

Eckhart Tolle, in his book, *A New Earth*, gives a simple explanation. He says we have two purposes:

"So the most important thing to remember is this: Your life has an inner purpose and an outer purpose. Inner purpose concerns Being and is primary. Outer purpose concerns doing and is secondary... Your inner purpose is to awaken. It is as simple as that. You share that purpose with every other person on the planet... Your outer purpose can change over time. It varies greatly from person to person."

Your outer purpose can be thought of as your *niche, role* or *story*. This can change over your lifetime, many times. And, it usually needs to be revamped when you transition to another stage in life.

In this book we are looking for your outer purpose—your story or niche in life right now. It involves knowing what you really want in life, your "true heart's desire".

Your outer purpose needs to align with your inner purpose in order for you to feel fulfilled and motivated to act. In other words, whatever work you are doing or role you are playing needs to have a higher calling that it is in agreement with.

This is where passion comes into play. When the two purposes are aligned you feel empowered and focused. Life becomes exciting and full of meaning. Your activities are deeply satisfying. You become like a laser beam instead of a light bulb.

"Knowing your purpose satisfies a deep need that lives in everyone: the need for meaning, to have a positive impact, to have your presence and life felt by others."

Tim Kelley—*True Purpose*

Niche

I love the word *niche* to describe your (outer) purpose in life. It conjures up a nice groove that you can just slot into where everything works and makes sense and rolls along smoothly. And, it's your niche and yours alone. It has your name on it.

Isn't that what we are all after? To find that nice groove in life that gives us confidence, a sense of place, and makes everything we do seem easy and effortless?

Life purpose sounds so grand, so huge, kind of overwhelming. It kind of cancels out those more mundane things we'd really love to do but that don't exactly shout life purpose. I had one client who really wanted to open a store, a little shop here in Mexico selling dolls. But she felt embarrassed because it wasn't *grand*.

Another client had always wanted to sell food—soups and stews—at a low price. She also felt it was somehow too hard to organize, but she loved to cook.

I want you to drop limiting ideas like these. Niche is what you'd love to do right now; it doesn't have to be an over-riding high-flown purpose. Heck, it can be needlepoint if that's what you love. Think small to start. You can always expand it if you need to.

It may be time to find a new niche in your life. So let's look at what you really want…

I Have No Idea What I Want!

Many of my clients say they have no idea what they really want to be doing with their lives. The frequent response to the question, what is it you really want, is, *"Well if I knew that I wouldn't have this problem, would I?"*

This is why it's so important to just relax and allow your goals to come to you. If you try to force them using mental power, it just won't work. They have to come from the heart. Cocooning and relaxing allows your subconscious mind to reveal them to you.

Finding true purpose, true heart's desire or simply one's role in life can seem like searching for the elusive Unicorn. Where do I look? What am I looking for, and how will I know when I've found it? Where do I start?

So, how *do* you find it? Where *do* you start? Robert Anthony, the personal development trainer, in his course *The Secret of Deliberate Creation*, says it's really quite easy. You start by asking yourself these questions:

"What would I like to have in my life that I don't have right now?"

"What are the consequences of not having it?"

"If I have it, how will it make me feel?"

"On a scale of 0—100, how much do I want it?"

(100 indicates a true heart's desire. Anything less is a wish. You are looking for 100s.)

Susan's Story

Susan moved to Mexico from Canada for the weather and the cheaper lifestyle. She was on a fixed income, handled her money well, and wanted to stretch it further than a life in Canada would allow. She was a true *Old Hippie at Heart*.

She had grown up on a farm and loved the outdoors. She craved warm weather all year long so she could indulge her passion for nature.

Susan was single and loved it. Everybody loved her and she was popular. She had children and grandchildren she visited regularly.

And, because she was healthy and vibrant, her friends came to rely on her. She had nursed several lonely people to their deaths because there was nobody else to do it. Other friends asked for her help in different areas. She was needed and busy but she wasn't totally at ease with her story.

She wasn't really a caretaker at heart and she valued her free time. She didn't have the *Caretaker* Archetype, and although content to do her duty and help out, didn't want to become a nursemaid for everyone.

When she was approaching 70 she became involved with friends who were passionate about creating a self-sustaining community in the Mexican countryside; she decided this was the next step for her. Susan wasn't totally convinced she would enjoy living so close to others all the time, commune style, but she loved the idea of living in the country, growing her own food and living an organic, sustainable lifestyle.

She was getting older—why not? So she signed up for the adventure. There would be no turning back; she would have to sink all her money into this project and it would be a permanent commitment. Like getting married. Maybe even more so.

The plan was to move in near her 70th birthday. However, when the time came, the new place wasn't ready and there was delay upon delay. Then she turned 70 and something shifted inside Susan. Wow. 70. She had truly entered a new era in her life and reconsidered her decision. Was this what she wanted? Truly? She examined her heart and realized it wasn't.

So she chose a new story to live by, one that would work for her. She dropped out of the project and moved out to the country into a beautiful little casita within striking distance of the commune, but far enough away to maintain her autonomy.

She wanted her own space, her independence. She wanted to do things her way.

She now travels a lot, visits her children regularly, comes into town when she feels like it, and the rest of the time enjoys herself on her own in the country. She spends her days pottering around in her organic garden, bird watching, cooking, listening to music, meditating, and painting. It's all on her time. These are her passions. She loves the land and working with her hands. She loves her art.

Her new story is—this is *my* time now. I'm not doing anything I don't want to do and am doing all the things I've always loved doing. She realized just in time that this was her true heart's desire and she created a story to build her new life around.

Your true heart's desire doesn't have to be on a grand scale. It can be gentle and totally personal, like Susan's.

Susan found her niche, her role, and it's one that suits her perfectly for this time in her life. As she tells her friends, she may change it tomorrow—there's no one to stop her!

More Purpose Questions

Tim Kelley in his book *True Purpose* encourages journaling to find your purpose. He gives a selection of questions designed to stimulate ideas about your passion and your calling.

"When are the times in your life when you've felt most passionate?"

"When are the times when you've felt most fulfilled?"

"When did you feel life had the most meaning?"

"When have you experienced flow?"

He recommends that you avoid including events like the birth of a child or a wedding in answering these questions, as these have universal significance and are not specific to you.

Flow

Mihaly Csikszentmihalyi is a Hungarian psychologist who is best known as the architect of the modern psychological concept of *flow*—the state of being totally absorbed in an activity.

He focuses on creativity and happiness, and his contention is that human beings are their happiest when in the state of *flow*.

You are in *flow* when you are engaged in an activity that is challenging and for which you have some skill. Where those two meet, you lose yourself, and time and ego disappear. You become totally absorbed; blissfully concentrated on the task at hand.

If an activity is too challenging, and your skill is not quite up to it, you get stressed or anxious. If it isn't challenging enough, you get bored.

Artists, musicians and athletes are all familiar with the *flow* state. I'm sure you are too. When you are in *flow* the unconscious mind takes over and rational thinking stops. You become unconsciously competent. It's the sweet spot, when you peak. You are inspired and unstoppable.

When have you been in flow?

Flow is not the same as relaxation or even bliss. It must have the element of challenge to qualify as *flow*. It is not the same as "going with the flow". Lying on the beach is not *flow*. Having a massage is not *flow*. Sorry, sex is not *flow*. These activities are enjoyable and relaxing, but don't fulfill the criteria for *flow*.

Flow is about challenge, purpose, total absorption and the absence of the chattering mind. It is pure concentration and focus.

Painting a picture, writing, making music, sports, cooking or public speaking can put you in *flow*.

Frequently when I write, I forget everything. It can be 3 in the afternoon and I've been writing for hours—I've forgotten to eat, to drink, to shower and I've lost all track of time. Yet I'm animated and full of energy as if I've been given a shot of adrenaline. This is *flow*.

Discover and remind yourself what causes you to be in flow. Recall times when you were totally fulfilled with what you were doing, so much so that you felt it was what you were put on earth to do. Excited, challenged, happy. This will be where your true heart's desire lies. If you want to have passion and juice in your life you must find what puts you in *flow*.

One day I was walking up one of San Miguel's many hills with my friend Andrea. We were both winded and panting when we reached the top. I reproached her, saying, *"You shouldn't be out of breath. You dance three times a week. You must be fit!"*

"When I dance, it's different" she replied. "I feel no tiredness, I never get out of breath, and my aches and pains disappear."

"Why is that?" I asked.

"Passion," she said.

Questions To Play With

Discovering what you really want:

What is the one thing you would do, if you knew you could not fail?

What would you do if money, time or energy were no object?

What would you want to accomplish if you knew you only had a year to live? 5 years?

Imagine you were told a magic Genie would give you the power to accomplish one great thing in your life if you would just identify it—what would it be?

130

Finding your areas of interest and skill:

What have you always been good at and easy for you?

What has always attracted your interest? What subjects at school and university?

What type of workshop or lecture are you always drawn to?

What subjects have you always had a secret interest in, but were reluctant for some reason to pursue?

If you could wave a magic wand and be really excellent at something, what would it be?

If you could give advice to your younger self about what directions to take in life, what would it be?

And then, the million-dollar question:

What is the one thing, if you could change it right now, that would make the most difference in your life?

Finding Your Flow:

When have you been in flow?

What activities cause you to be in flow?

What activity totally absorbs you?

When have you been so totally immersed in something that you forgot to eat or drink or rest? And, you felt high as a kite afterwards?

Explore all these questions. Some of them may resonate, and I suspect at least one of them will hold the key to your true longings and desires.

Write down your answers.

What patterns do you see?

What do these answers point to as your true heart's desire?

Let's Review

Finding your purpose, your true heart's desire, is crucial for living with passion.

We have two purposes—an inner and an outer purpose. The inner purpose we share with everyone and that is to awaken and become conscious. The outer purpose is unique to each individual and is about your niche or role in life.

Finding your outer purpose involves knowing yourself and being authentic. It involves asking yourself searching questions to uncover what you deeply desire, what your interests and skills are and what puts you in *flow*—the state of being totally and blissfully absorbed in an activity.

When you feel you have an idea of what you truly want in life you will feel an emotional resonance. It will feel right, it will feel exciting, and it will be motivating and inspiring.

Now it's time for the next part of the journey, which is about defining your niche and rewriting your story. Let's move on!

Chapter 10

"Both Sides, Now":
Writing Your New Life Story

"Each of us has two distinct choices to make about what we will do with our lives. The first choice we can make is to be less than we have the capacity to be. To earn less, to have less, to read less and to think less. To try less and discipline ourselves less. These are the choices that lead to an empty life. These are the choices that, once made, lead to a life of constant apprehension instead of a life of wondrous anticipation. And the second choice? To do it all! To become all that we can possibly be. To read every book that we possibly can. To earn as much as we possibly can. To give and share as much as we possibly can. To strive and produce and accomplish as much as we possibly can."

Jim Rohn

By now, if you've gotten this far, answered the questions and experimented with the techniques, I imagine you are beginning to

133

have an inkling of who you could be and what you could really accomplish in life. I'm hoping it feels exciting, maybe even a little scary, and you are beginning to ask yourself, *"What if I could...have that dream, achieve that goal, write that book, start that charity, take up sailing...? Why not me?"*

What would you do if you knew you couldn't fail?

In this chapter you are going to pull together all the bits and pieces that you have discovered—all the gems, the treasure—and shape them into your role, your niche and your purpose for your life right now. You can look at your life from both sides, now, and can rewrite your life script, from a new perspective.

What you need to look at now are the special circumstances of your life, at this particular moment, which will have a bearing on what is going to fulfill you and give your life meaning.

Creating A Dream Recipe

You can create a new recipe, a new combination of ingredients, that's going to work perfectly for you at this stage in your life.

Take time now, after you've answered the questions in the preceding chapter, to reflect and meditate on what you have discovered about yourself up to this point.

Your new recipe needs practical ingredients and some big dollops of dreaming.

The ingredients in your recipe:

First of all, allow yourself to daydream.

If you could wave a magic wand and create your perfect life, how would it be?

What would your perfect life look like? What would you be doing? How would you spend your time?

134

What would a perfect day, a perfect week, look like?

Allow your dreaming to be as crazy and unrealistic as it wants to be. Just let your imagination flow and reveal to you how you would ideally like to spend your time. Would you love to be an expert on the stock market? A renowned artist? A best selling author? A TV cook? A travel writer? A charity organizer?

Don't allow your inner critic (the Saboteur!) to question how you could make this happen. The reality check can come later. For now, what would you really love to do if you had no restrictions?

Write this down. This is the first ingredient of the recipe.

The rest of the ingredients:

Now we need to mix in some other important ingredients. You have in mind what you would really love to do and it's starting to feel good!

Look at your life situation, where you are living, your lifestyle, your health and your financial situation. These all need to go into the mix. This is where we get practical.

We are bringing your dreams down into the physical world and making them realistic. We are instigating a reality check that we hope doesn't spoil the flavor.

Financial:

If you need money, then your dream needs to take that into account. It's no good swanning off into the sunset in your metaphorical hippie van if you have nothing to live on.

How can I incorporate making money into my dream right now?

Energy:

Your energy and health are another consideration. My father is an example of the dangers of not taking your health into account. He was 65 and had heart trouble. Heading off to Kathmandu, high up in the Himalayas, was perhaps not the wisest choice.

If your energy and health are not what they used to be, then you need to factor that into your dream mix. Don't feel you have to pretend.

What can I do that will take into account my health and stamina?

Time:

How do you like to spend your time? Do you want to be busy? If you don't want too many restrictions on your time, include this in your mix. As you get older, or after you retire, you may relish lots of free time. I like my afternoons free. And mornings too, actually...

How do I want to spend my days? How much free time do I want?

How can I balance my purposeful activities and my free time to meet all my needs?

Challenge level:

Do you relish challenge in your life, or do you prefer a stress-free existence? You may have had enough stress in your past and now just want something to do that you enjoy and that feels easy and effortless. I find I'm not happy or in *flow* without a little challenge. I want something to keep me on my toes, but not stressed. What feels right for you?

How much stress am I willing to have in my life right now? Appointments? Responsibilities?

136

How much challenge do I need in order to stay interested and engaged?

People:

Who do you want to fulfill your purpose with? Are there other people who need to be involved in your dream life? Do you need a coach to help you? (I did)

In the *Hero's Journey*, the hero eventually comes across a mentor or guide to help him, or her, find the missing piece that completes the search. Remember Yoda in Star Wars? Star Wars is based on the *Hero's Journey*. It is peopled with Archetypes too.

Everyone needs some help along the way, whether a coach, a trusted friend, a mentor, a therapist or a counselor. You need someone who will give you objective advice and push you to be the best you can be.

Most successful people have a coach. Even great spiritual masters start with a teacher who shows them their path.

Who do I need to bring into my life to help me find my purpose?

Who do I need to help me fulfill my purpose?

Where do I need to look to find my mentor?

Resources:

What resources do you need to make your dream come true?

Financial resources? New skills? An assistant? A new office or computer?

Decide what you will need to make your dream into reality. It may be that seminar in Hawaii you've been drooling over, or renovating your spare room into an office or workroom.

What do I need in my life, that I don't have right now, to make my dreams come true?

What do I need to learn to bring these things into my life?

What is the one skill, that if I learned it well, would make the most difference to me?

Whatever You Come Up With Is Perfect!

Combine all these ingredients and see what you come up with. You may already have a clear idea of something you would love to do and are raring to go.

Great! It's exciting, isn't it? Do you feel a great *whoosh* of energy when you think about it?

For some people, the answer to what they want to do with their lives can come all of a sudden, in one go, just by answering the recipe questions.

For me, on the other hand, it came in a series of increments. Little by little I honed my ideas until finally, one day, talking with my coach, I had an "aha" moment and everything became crystal clear. But this was after months of working on it and answering the questions posed in this book, dozens of times.

Combining the ingredients. Tasting the recipe. Adding something, taking something away. Getting it right. Working on it.

Miguel's Story

Miguel was a Mexican from Chihuahua who was a successful self-made businessman. He retired and went back to Mexico, after an intense and dynamic career in the States. He had worked hard, achieved a lot, and at this point wanted to enjoy the fruits of his efforts.

He had no financial need to work anymore.

He allowed himself to cocoon in his new home, enjoying the weather and the tranquil environment. He didn't rush to create a new story, but he instinctively knew he was going to need a new paradigm to live by to fully enjoy his new situation.

He enjoyed not having full time responsibilities around work, but he missed feeling part of things, feeling involved, being a player.

After a while he built himself an office next to his house, and above it a meditation room. He knew what his true heart's desire was—meditation, spiritual study and yoga, without interruption. He spent his mornings in his meditation room. Soon he started a meditation group that met twice weekly. People just started gravitating to him to learn meditation techniques.

It wasn't long before people from his old company started coming to see him at his office. They wanted his help and advice with their work. He was asked to train and give talks, and eventually he became busy again. This time it was at his pace, and he made sure he kept most of his mornings free for meditation and yoga, and also time to swim.

He became a sort of "elder statesman" in his company, being asked to speak in many different places about how he had achieved his success. He had a ready-made platform to share how meditation had been a key element in his business success. He embraced his new role and indulged his passions at the same time. He created a new story for himself in retirement—one that built on his strengths, combining his interests and skills as well as his true heart's desires.

He rewrote his script for living. He changed his myth and found the perfect mix. But it was the cocooning, the relaxing, that enabled everything to fall into place.

Rewrite Your Myth

We each have a myth or story we are living by. This myth is a combination of beliefs about our abilities, how the world works, our roles in life, our expectations, and our personal circumstances.

Myths provide us with guideposts for living.

Our myths sometimes need rewriting when circumstances change and when we enter new eras in our lives. If we try to live an outdated myth we may become frustrated and stuck.

There are certain events in life that we would do well to look out for—ones that are warning signs that we are going to need to revisit our myth and rewrite our story.

Retirement: Your job frequently provides you with a tribe to identify with. When you are no longer working at your job or career, you lose a role and part of your identity.

Children leaving home: You may need a role change if being a parent was a big part of who you were and how you spent your time.

Death of someone close to you: When you lose someone close to you, it may involve reorienting your life, where you live, and your day to day activities.

New partner or spouse: It's essential to write a new story. You can't live the life you had with your former partner or when living alone. This is a brand new role for you.

Moving: If you have moved, especially to a different country, all the physical aspects of your life change. You definitely can't live as if you are in the old country. Even moving house may require a rewrite.

Hitting a new decade: If your next birthday has a zero in it, you may find this disconcerting. For many, entering a new decade is a wake-up call and a time to revisit their life and goals.

You may have different reasons for needing to change your story. Any transition or change in your life can precipitate the need for a rethink about your life.

What Is Your Myth?

Identify the myth you are living by. Think of old myths and legends. Think of fairy tales and classic stories. Does your life remind you of a cliché, like a horse put out to pasture? What is your life *like*?

In my case, I met my new husband while facing some financial problems after my divorce. He came into my life like a *Knight in Shining Armor* and rescued me. I was playing the role of the quintessential *Damsel in Distress*. Certainly I was in financial distress.

We eventually moved to Mexico and got married. I had no more financial worries and felt protected and looked after.

I became…the Princess in the Ivory Tower!

Have you ever wondered what becomes of those princesses in fairy tales after they marry their prince? They get bored! What do you do all day in a tower? I didn't even have to keep it clean and tidy. I no longer had to compete in the world of business, as I had for many years. I no longer had children to look after and I no longer had to pay any bills. What was my new role? *Lazy Princess*!

So what was I to do when I had no responsibilities? Get my hair done? Lunch with friends? Well, that was fun for a while and then I became very restless.

A Princess Rewrites Her Story

So how does a *Princess* rewrite her story, and find a new fairy tale to live by? I had to come down out of the tower and go out hunting for my purpose. I had to engage with the real world again.

I brought my *Warrior* in from pasture to help me. I roused my *Old Hippie at Heart* from slumber.

I began my Hero's Journey with my coach as Mentor, and started working with my archetypes: Business Woman, Rebel, Seeker, Writer, Coach, Teacher, Pioneer, Warrior, Student, Old Hippie.

I reconnected with my passions—writing, coaching, and hypnotherapy. I realized I wanted to help others who were going through transitions like I had, and to help my fellow Boomers learn how to age fearlessly and defiantly. I learned that in order to help others heal, I had to heal myself first. I had to face *my* demons, if I wanted to help others face *their* demons.

I couldn't help others when I was still wandering in the forest.

I cleared my agenda; much as I enjoyed Pilates, Spanish classes (not really), art and cooking classes, those activities filled up my days and left me no time for anything else. If I wanted to write, I needed some totally free days in my week.

Then I went and took an advanced course in hypnotherapy in northern California. It was bliss…interesting, challenging, and got me back in the saddle. Sometimes you need to do some training in your field of interest, if only to convince yourself that you are on the right track. Ongoing training can provide a great boost in confidence. I'm a big fan, but then I would be, because I'm the *Eternal Student!*

Now I write and work in the mornings and play in the afternoons. This way I still have plenty of time for lunch with friends. That's one activity I haven't stopped. When I lived in England, everyone worked full time and lunch was expensive. In Houston, lunch with friends was impossible, as everybody lived an hour away.

Here in San Miguel, lunch is no more than 7 minutes away and costs no more than the equivalent of $5 or $6. This is a "make-friends" town and everybody loves to meet in the numerous charming and inexpensive sidewalk cafes. So lunch? Coffee? Sure—I'm available. Just say where and I'm there.

Still maintaining a little time for some of those *Princess* activities. This is *my* recipe after all. Create yours to fit you.

Questions To Explore

What ingredients need to go into your recipe for a new story, a new role in life?

Money

Health

Time

Challenge level

People

Resources

Taking all these elements into consideration, what activities come to mind?

What do you really want to be doing with your time?

What would you do if money, time, energy level, or age, was no object?

What would you do if you knew you couldn't fail?

Rewriting your story, changing your myth:

How would you describe your life right now?

Is it working for you?

How did it work for you before?

Is it time to change? What would be a great and exciting new story?

What archetypes do you need to bring into your new story?

I needed to bring my Warrior out of retirement to get me back into the world as a player again. I also needed to reawaken my Pioneer and my Old Hippie at Heart. Maybe you need an Artist? A Muse? A Sage? A Guru? A King? What about a Disciplinarian?

What ideally would you want to be doing with your life. What niche would really work for you?

How does this make you feel when you think about it?

If you feel excited, passionate and motivated, you have hit the jackpot!

Now, let's take the final step. The hero has to return home at some point. Traditionally in the legends, the hero is somewhat reluctant to return to the real world. The journey is so exciting! So. What now? Back in the van, we're heading towards home.

Chapter 11

"Stairway to Heaven": Manifest Your Dreams & Create Your New Life

"Imagine for a moment
your own version of a perfect future.
See yourself in that future
with everything you could wish for
at this very moment fulfilled.
Now take the memory of that future
and bring it here into the present.
Let it influence how you will behave
from this moment on."

Deepak Chopra

The Hero's Return

Now it's time to return from your *Hero's Journey* and manifest your newfound purpose.

For me, this is the fun part. You're going to make it all happen.

A fully realized, authentic individual, living with purpose, whose life has meaning and passion, is a person who will automatically feel happy. Or to put it another way, a person who will be too involved and busy to worry about whether they are happy or not.

Your New Ideas

If you have gotten this far in the book, I imagine you are full of new ideas, and I trust your creative juices are flowing. You feel some inspiration, something that has got you out of the dark forest you've been wandering in.

If not, then go back and cocoon for awhile. You may still need to complete that part of the process.

Can you remember feeling inspired and pumped up before, from reading a book perhaps, or attending a seminar? Then, a few days later, the motivation to do something new had disappeared. I'm guessing you really don't want that to happen again.

It's easy to get fired up and excited, isn't it? However, it's not so easy to carry through and actually get something to happen as a result.

This is partly to do with the subconscious mind's natural resistance to change.

It's also the work of our "friend" the *Saboteur*, who is determined to stop us from making changes.

It's also inertia. Homeostasis. An airplane requires the most fuel when it is taking off. A huge expenditure of energy is needed to get the plane off the ground. But once the plane is in the air, it needs relatively little fuel to keep going. In the same way, for you to do something different, to move out of your comfort zone, will require a lot of effort at the beginning.

So to get this dream going, to get out of your "slough of despond", you need to do something new and different. Soon. Now.

Now is the *only* time to do what you've always wanted to do. If not now, when? The advantage of getting older is developing a devil-may-care attitude. Who cares what anyone else thinks at this point? Start to live your dream and do it now!

Ask yourself these questions:

"What am I willing to change in order to have my dream?"

"What am I willing to give up, to sacrifice?"

Time spent on the Internet? TV? Sleeping? Playing Bridge? Drinking? A disempowering relationship? Bingo?

"What habits do I need to change?"

"What new skills do I need to learn?"

Chances are you can answer these questions straight away if you're being honest with yourself.

Creating Your Dream Life

There is a plethora of books and workshops available on goal setting and manifesting. The movie The Secret spawned an industry around the Law of Attraction, the idea that says what you focus on, think about and talk about, you will inevitably draw into your life.

People have always been fascinated with how to create the life they desire and attract the things they want. Shamans and healers, writers, spiritual leaders, marketing gurus, politicians, coaches, doctors and personal development trainers all appeal to the universal desire people have to make changes and to create a better life than the one they have now.

I think I've read most of the books on manifesting and the Law of Attraction. My shelves and my Kindle are stocked with various books on how to manifest a life you love. I've been fascinated, no *obsessed*, with goal setting and manifesting for years.

To me this is where the rubber meets the road. If what someone is teaching—whether an energy medicine technique, a new

147

religion, or the Law of Attraction—cannot produce positive, observable results in someone's life, then what is the point of it?

That applies to what I'm writing here too…

I will share with you some of what I've experienced, learned and achieved along the way to manifesting my ideal life.

Let me start by saying that I have been able to get manifesting to work extremely well for me. But it wasn't easy straight away and I really have to work on it. I have manifested many amazing things in my life and am very grateful for the life I'm living now in San Miguel, a gorgeous little paradise in the mountains of Mexico. I deeply enjoy living here.

My Obsession With Manifesting

I think my real obsession with manifesting began back when I was living in England; I was pulling away from my business training career and starting out as a budding coach and hypnotherapist, bumping along with a few clients, but with no real momentum.

One day I went to a well-known acupuncturist for a niggling, but not serious problem with my back. I arrived at his clinic and was impressed with how beautiful, peaceful and inviting it was. It was in an old English Victorian mansion, with beautiful gardens, high ceilings, old fireplaces—oh, the atmosphere was incredible.

I remember thinking, "*someone has manifested all this, the ambience, the beauty, the feeling of tranquility. It didn't happen by accident*". The waiting room was full— obviously business was good. I was looking forward to meeting the person who had created this lovely space.

When I met him, he didn't disappoint; in fact he knocked my socks off. He was a whirlwind of energy, success and charisma; dynamic, pony-tailed, enthusiastic, a little eccentric and obviously very good at what he did.

After that first session, I told a friend that I would give anything to be able to practice my hypnotherapy in his clinic. Just to soak up the vibes would be wonderful, not to mention the prestige! To receive clients in such a place would be amazing!

She suggested I make it happen by manifesting and visualizing him asking me to work there. I had never done this before but decided to give it a whirl.

Every day I affirmed that he was asking me to work there. I imagined exactly how it would happen.

During the next month of acupuncture sessions he and I chatted and he asked me about my work. I explained my philosophy of healing and change work and how I dealt with various clients.

On my last visit, he asked me to sit down for a moment before I left. Then he said, "I've been wanting a hypnotherapist working here to complete our staff—how would you feel about doing your work here from now on?"

I went cold, my mind went blank, my mouth dry, and time stood still. I felt dizzy. I did manage to croak out a *"yes, please, that would be great"* before I stumbled out the door.

It happened exactly as I imagined it would. I was *hooked* on manifesting.

I had a wonderful time in the clinic and I never lacked for clients. My clients loved working with me in that beautiful place and I remember my experiences there with pleasure.

That was my first taste of manifesting, but certainly not my last. It started me on my quest for the best ways to create and attract what you want into your life.

What I want to share with you now are the results of reading hundreds of books, attending numerous workshops and seminars, and years of experimenting.

I believe that I manifested everything I have in my life right now; my house, being married, the pool, and my friends, and even my Chihuahua. I thought them up first!

I wanted a cat and Lucy arrived soon after and graced me with her presence. A gorgeous street cat, she must have heard through the universal grapevine that I needed her.

I'm almost convinced I manifested San Miguel de Allende, the beautiful Mexican town where I live, because before I knew anything about it, I imagined a town exactly like it. It is perfect for me.

Let me share how I get manifesting to work.

Goal Setting and Manifesting

Let's look at the difference between goal setting and manifesting. Some people confuse the two. Although they are related, they are different processes. Each is important in creating your ideal life. I will describe how I use these two processes so you can understand the differences.

Goal setting involves deciding what you want as specifically as possible, even setting a time limit on it, and then writing it down. It is essential for getting really clear and focused about what you want, and the things you want to change in your life.

Goal setting works well when you know exactly what you want, especially for material goals and specific things you want to accomplish.

For example, if you want a new car, or to lose weight or learn a new language, it works well. You have clear objectives. It also works well with financial matters and if you have a time limit for when you need something done.

These are *specific* areas or *specific* material things that you want for a *specific* time.

SMART Goals

S.M.A.R.T is an acronym for the requirements for creating a clear goal. It is a well-known process to ensure your goal is well formed, realistic and focused.

The requirements for defining your goal are:

Specific—What, where, who, is involved in this goal? What will it look like? Who is involved? Where will it take place?

Measurable—How will you know when you've achieved it? What will have changed?

Achievable—Is this goal realistic? Do you actually believe you can do it? (Belief is a huge element of motivation.)

Resources—What resources—people, new skills, money—do you need to achieve this goal? How will you get them? What is your plan?

Time bound—When do you want this goal? (If you don't set a time on it, it could take place in the far distant future.)

Using the **SMART** goals process is essential for engaging the conscious mind and establishing buy-in to your goal. You need to have your conscious mind accept that a goal is possible, do-able and within your reach. Making your goals **SMART** ensures that acceptance.

The process will also identify and uncover any unconscious obstacles to achieving your goal.

For example, making the goal measurable can sometimes be challenging. How do you measure learning a language? You need to set very specific measures for what you want to achieve and when. Learning a language is an ongoing process—you're never "there". So to make this goal **SMART** you need to break it down into measurable chunks that your mind can grasp and feel comfortable with.

If your goal isn't measurable, your unconscious mind may not understand what you are aiming for. If your goal isn't achievable or

151

realistic (I want to earn a million dollars in the next 3 months) your unconscious mind may just turn off in regard to it. And, if you can't define it specifically, you may not be able to visualize it.

These are all obstacles that can prevent your success. The **SMART** process uncovers them so you can deal with them.

Additional Goal Setting Ingredients

In addition to being **SMART**, goals need the "three **Ps**": to be stated in the **positive**, in the **present** tense and be totally **personal** to you. These are the same rules that apply to affirmations, which we discussed in Chapter 4. I will repeat those rules here for emphasis.

1) State your goal in the **present** tense as if it is already achieved. *"I am X..."* rather than *"I will X..."* "I will" puts your goal forever in the future.

2) State your goal in **positive** language. Do not focus on what you are trying to get rid of. State *"I am my perfect weight"* rather than *"I am no longer fat"*.

The unconscious mind processes in images; therefore, if you state the latter, it will visualize fat and may create more of it. That, you do not want.

The unconscious mind is keen to carry out your wishes, so be careful what you tell it and what pictures you are creating for it. It will do as it is instructed.

3) Make sure your goal is **personal** to you and not a goal for someone else. Use lots of *I am...I have...or I allow myself...*statements. These statements avoid resistance or negative reactions.

152

You can end your affirmation or goal statement with powerful phrases such as "*I am now instructing my unconscious mind to assist me in making these changes right now*". Personal development trainer Robert Anthony likes to finish affirmations with the command, *"Make it so!"* from Star Trek.

Motivation—The Secret Ingredient

Another important aspect of goal achieving is motivation. If you have motivation, a burning desire for something, you can make it happen, and it can seem easy.

Without motivation, it's an uphill struggle.

"When you know what you want, and you want it badly enough, you'll find a way to get it."

Jim Rohn

Let's look at several aspects of motivation.

Benefits—what you are really after

Now I'll show you a technique that will make you really clear about *why* you want the goal and will help you get that burning desire. Take a piece of paper and fold it down the middle. At the top of the page write your goal. Then at the top of one column write, "The benefits of having this goal" and at the top of the other column write, "The consequences of not having this goal".

List as many answers as you can think of. Write rapidly and don't *over* think it. This will help you establish your *towards* and *away-from* motivations for the goal. It's ok to have more benefits than consequences, but it's generally not so good to have more consequences. If that is the case, keep working on the benefits.

Now take one of your benefits and ask yourself, *"if I have this, what will this do for me?"* Then, take that answer and ask, *"and if I*

153

have that, what will that do for me? " Keep asking until you get to an emotion or value such as peace, joy, love, contentment, happiness, or feeling good about yourself.

The highest benefit of all goals is a positive emotion. Therefore the emotion is your true goal. Always. The stated goal is simply a way to have that emotion.

You can choose to have that emotion now. Just imagine you have it right now and notice how good that feels. This will help you achieve your goal.

Visualize it

Now take your goal and ask yourself how you will know when it has happened. What will be different in your life when you have achieved your goal? You already know how you want to feel but what will be going on in your life? How will things have changed for you?

After all, if nothing will change, then it's not a goal. A goal involves change.

So how will you know when you're there with your goal? What will prove it for you? For instance it may be stepping on the scales and seeing a certain weight. It may be gaining a certificate— walking up on the stage and hearing the applause. It may be hearing yourself chatting away in your new language.

Maybe somebody is asking you what you've done because you're looking so young?

Where will you be? Who will be there? What is happening? What are you hearing? What are you feeling? When will this be happening?

Take a moment to be by yourself and close your eyes. Imagine you are watching a video of yourself having achieved your goal and notice what is going on; what you are saying to yourself or what others are saying to you, what is happening around you and what you are doing.

Now step into the video, into your body, looking out of your own eyes; feel the emotions and experience it fully.

This should make you feel excited about your goal. It should feel good in the pit of your stomach and in your heart. Your gut instincts should tell you it's right. Put your hands on each of these parts of your body, state your goal and notice how you feel.

If it doesn't feel totally right, you may need to go back around the loop again, making it **SMART,** and asking all the questions until you get it to feel right.

The positive emotions are where your motivation lies.

Do the visualizing at least twice a day until you either achieve your goal or it no longer excites you. That is a sign you need to change the visual, to switch it up until it motivates you again. Or reconsider your goal and your motivations. Sometimes we simply need to change the goal, or it may be time to just release and let it go. Your work is done.

Sometimes we find we no longer want that goal. That's ok too. Don't cling to a goal simply because at one time you wanted it. There are times we need to let go. Just let it go—accept that your life has changed and that you have evolved. It may be that you no longer need that goal in your life.

Planning and Action

Tony Robbins in his book, Awaken the Giant Within, says, "All goal setting must immediately be followed by the development of a plan, and massive and consistent action towards its fulfillment."

The most effective way to keep your motivation alive is to take action.

Make a list of some action steps you can take *right away* to further your new goals and to create a life filled with purpose.

Action produces results and results produce momentum. Momentum creates motivation.

Tony goes on to say that he constantly asks himself—"what would I want for my life if I knew I could have it any way I wanted it? What would I go for if I knew I could not fail?"

These are truly million dollar questions. They have certainly made Tony a millionaire many times over.

Goal achieving needs action, discipline and perseverance. The Law of Attraction is not about just visualizing, then sitting around and waiting for your ideal life to materialize. While you wait, you need to get busy.

Taking action signals to the Universe that you are serious about what you want. It will sit up and pay attention and then help you make it happen.

Action activates the Law of Attraction.

Manifesting

Manifesting is related to, but slightly different from goal setting. It is about making changes and having something different come into your life, but it is more magical, more mysterious, than goal setting.

You can manifest anything—it doesn't have to be personal, specific, achievable or realistic. You don't necessarily need to take action. It doesn't need to be **SMART.**

Manifesting is the arena of miracles. You can manifest wonderful things for other people as well as yourself. The stairway to heaven…

Manifesting is more like daydreaming than goal setting. You just let your mind go into a trance and imagine what you'd really love to happen. It's about creating your ideal life without knowing exactly what that would entail.

It works when you *don't* know specifically what you want and you *can't* see it yet in your mind's eye.

For example, a few months back I started manifesting a roof garden for my house. We have a lovely flat roof, with steps up to it, where we can sit and watch the sunset over the Sierra Madre Mountains. But I never enjoyed being up there much because the roof area just didn't look very pretty. We had a few chairs up there but that was all. It was kind of bleak.

I kept thinking how nice it would be if it were fixed up. However, I couldn't visualize it because I really didn't know how it should look. I had no idea how to design a roof garden or even what I actually wanted.

So I just started affirming to myself, "I have a wonderful new roof garden. It pleases me and I enjoy sitting there. I feel great about it. When I'm up there and I look around, I love the way it looks".

I have a new garden now and it's nothing like I would have imagined it. It just kind of evolved; everything fell into place in its own time, the furniture, the tiles. And it's perfect. I now watch the sunrise as well as the sunset in the mountains. I have a 360-degree view. Plush sofas to dream on.

Manifesting *assumes* the Universe can create something better than you can imagine, and who wants to mess with that? It takes trust and patience and allowing things to unfold, as they will. I know some people regard this as a bit wacky, but probably not if you are an *Old Hippie at Heart*. We are sort of wacky.

Just try it and see.

My Preferred Method of Manifesting

I have found that making statements about what I want to happen works best for me. For example, before I moved to San Miguel I would say to myself, "*I am living in a house I love, and that my children love visiting. It has a pool. I am happily married and have many friends and interesting ways to spend my time. I love where I live and I love my life."*

I didn't "see" the house, the pool, the wedding. I didn't know what they would look like or how I wanted them to be. I just stated my intentions, many times. Then I imagined how nice that felt. I also added the statement from Shakti Gawain's book *Creative Visualization, "This or something better is now coming to me in totally satisfying and harmonious ways for the highest good of all concerned."*

I surrounded my intentions with feelings of bliss, peace and contentment.

Then I let them go. I didn't keep revisiting them. Like planting seeds, if you dig them up to see how they are doing, they won't grow into plants.

All of this came to pass in ways I could never have imagined.

So to reiterate, my favorite and most effective way to manifest is this:

1) **Daydream** what your ideal life would be like. Imagine yourself in 6 months or a year. *What is it you don't have right now that you would like to have? What would you like to accomplish? How would you like your life to be?*

2) Now, just **imagine you are living** in this dream. Imagine how great it feels. *How are you feeling? What are you doing? How are you spending your time?*

3) Then just **state it as if it is happening already**. Write it down and date it. (It's fun to look back and see when you wrote it.) Don't worry about seeing it clearly. I suggest you don't try to fill in too many details. Simply have a general idea of what you would like and how you would like to feel when it happens.

4) **Notice how you feel** when you think about it. Do you feel good? Are the emotions positive? Imagine surrounding the ideas with bliss.

5) **Release it** and let it go. You can revisit it now and then, but don't cling to the results. Just trust and have patience that your intentions will manifest exactly how and when they are supposed to.

Manifesting is appropriate when you are not exactly sure what you want or when you want it. It may be something for someone else. It's about designing a life.

Have Fun With This

Goal setting:

1) Ask yourself these questions:

What am I willing to change in order to have my dream?

What am I willing to give up, to sacrifice? What habits?

What needs to be different in my life?

2) Take your goals through the **SMART** process. Make them

Specific

Measurable

Achievable

Resourced

Timed

3) Answer these questions:

Is my goal statement present tense, positive and personal to me?

If your motivation isn't sufficiently burning, tweak your goal until it's more exciting for you.

Take a sheet of paper, write your goal at the top, fold it down the middle and at the top of one column write "the benefits of having this goal" and at the top of the other column, "the consequences of not having this goal". Write your answers.

After each benefit, ask what that will do for you. Keep asking until you reach a positive emotion such as peace, love, joy, contentment or feeling good about myself. That is your true goal.

4) Now imagine you already have your goal.

What is different?

What has changed in my life?

How would I like it to be?

How am I feeling?

Take a few moments every day to imagine yourself having already achieved your goal. Imagine you are watching a video, see who is there, what is being said and what you are feeling. Now step into the video, into your own body and experience it fully.

5) Now take action. What is the first thing you need to do? Do it!

Manifesting:

If your goal is more suitable for manifesting because you're not sure of what you want, or it's for someone else and not you, then daydream about what you would like to happen. It could be about your whole lifestyle. You can be vague and unspecific.

1) **Daydream** what your ideal life would be like. What is it you don't have that you would like to have? What would you like to accomplish? How would you like it to be? Imagine yourself in 6 months or a year. How are you feeling?

2) Now, just **imagine** you are living your dream, your purpose. Imagine how great that feels.

3) Then just **state it** as if it is happening already. Write it down and date it. It's fun to look back. Don't worry about seeing it clearly. I suggest you don't try to fill in details. Simply have a general idea of what you would like and how you would feel when it happens.

4) Notice how you feel when you think about it. **Do you feel good**? Are the emotions positive? Imagine surrounding the ideas with bliss.

5) **Release it** and don't cling to it. You can revisit it now and then, but don't cling to the results. Just trust and have patience that your intentions will manifest exactly how and when they are supposed to.

Make a manifesting statement that describes what you want to happen. Use "I am" statements and put emotion into it. "I am living in a house I love, and that my children love visiting. It has a pool. I am happily married and have many friends and activities. I love where I live and I love my life."

Hey, I think we're just about done! Time to live the rest of your life…

Chapter 12

"It's the Springtime of My Life..."

"My father learned the French language at 65 years of age, and became an authority on it at 70. He made a study of Gaelic when he was over 60, and became an acknowledged and famous teacher of the subject. He passed away at 99...his handwriting, and his reasoning powers had improved with age. Truly, you are as old as you think and feel."

Joseph Murphy—*The Power of Your Subconscious Mind*

Your age *never, ever, ever* should prevent you from living your ideal life, creating goals, and doing what you've always wanted to do. It is never an excuse to stop pushing back against what other people expect of you rather than doing what you want to do.

It's *never, ever* too late to live the life you were meant to live. Even though that's a cliché, it is still true. There are countless examples of people getting into their stride and finding themselves late in life, after 60, even after 70, and even after 80 or 90. It's called being a late bloomer.

Alfred Tennyson wrote a magnificent poem, *Crossing the Bar*, at 83. Isaac Newton was hard at work close to 85. At 88 John Wesley was directing, preaching and guiding Methodism. Grandma Moses started painting in her 60s and became world famous.

George Bernard Shaw was active at 90, and the artistic quality of his mind had not diminished in the slightest.

To me, these examples are inspiring and motivating. Life can just get better and better as you age.

It's Never Too Late

"Get it out of your head once and for all that 65, 75, or 85 years of age is synonymous with the end for you or anybody else. It can be the beginning of a glorious, fruitful, active and most productive life pattern, better than you have ever experienced. Believe this, expect it and your subconscious will bring it to pass."

Joseph Murphy—*The Power of Your Subconscious Mind*

Let's face it, getting older can be disconcerting at any age. Do you remember approaching 30? How ancient it felt? Turning 30 seemed like the end of youth in many ways.

Then there was turning 40. Oh dear. I remember applying for jobs at 39. I felt mortified that I was nearly 40 and was embarrassed to put my age down on applications, thinking that I would be passed over automatically. I probably was. That was a while back.

Several decades later, 39 sounds like a baby to me. It just illustrates my point—that whatever age you are, it feels like you're getting old because it's *the oldest you've ever been.* For some reason the birthdays with zeros in them cause us to feel our age the most, to sit up and take notice.

The start of a new decade feels like entering a new era of life and it sounds *so much older* than the decade before.

What helps you keep perspective is to imagine you're zooming out years into the future and looking back on you, now, and giving your present self advice and encouragement. What would you be proud of? What regrets would you have? What one piece of advice would you give yourself from an older perspective? It's not too late to change and to enact that advice!

Recently I asked a client to do this. She was dissatisfied with a life which was filled with Mahjong and social activities. When she went out into the future and looked back, the first thing she said was, *"well, I don't regret not playing another game of Mahjong!"*

I doubt I would regret not being one more hour on Facebook. My father wrote himself a message a few days before he died: "spend less time reading newspapers!"

Joan Rivers, the comedienne, is still going strong at 80. She works harder and has more energy than many 20 year olds. She recently won *Celebrity Apprentice* against hot, and much younger, competition. Nobody has told her she ought to slow down and act her age. If they have, she's obviously ignored them.

(Joan recently died during an operation. She was at the top of her game and sorely missed by many.)

I urge you to focus on role models that inspire you and look for role models for inspiration. Inspiration is everywhere if you open up to it.

For example, the other day my older sister mentioned she had been invited to the celebration of a friend who had just earned his Ph.D. in Marine Biology…at age 69. Wow. I didn't know any other details but that information was enough to let my imagination play. Starting afresh, at age 69, with a new career. I loved it. What kind of mindset, what beliefs would he have needed to enable him to accomplish this? I want some of that!

Stories like this show up every day. People in the third stage of life, including *Old Hippies,* are a force to be reckoned with! We are pushing the envelope and creating new paradigms when and where we need them.

I collect stories like these in my mind for encouragement and inspiration. Too many people feel they have to give up their dreams when they hit the young age of 60. These days it's just not true!

Design your life purpose with things you can do at any age—art, music, writing, coaching, healing, charity work, interior design, gardening, pie-making, photography, working with animals, marine biology, and oh, don't forget Internet businesses. These activities don't have age constraints.

What is it you always wanted to do? It's not too late to do it now…and seriously, what better time is there?

I love doing NLP, working as a Life Coach and Hypnotherapist. I love writing. I love presenting workshops. And as long as I am physically able, there is no reason I can't continue doing these things right up until my dotage. I love the idea of being in my 90s, surrounded by my animals, still dispensing advice—whether wanted or not!

Meditation

No book on alternative ways of aging would be complete without a section on meditation. Deepak Chopra, the celebrity doctor, writer and inspirational mentor of the human potential movement, says it is "the most important activity we can do to keep young and active." He cites research that strongly suggests meditation keeps both the mind and body young and actually *reverses* the signs of aging.

There is not room here to explore all the different ways to meditate. There are hundreds of methods to choose from. I have

166

been meditating for 10 years. It has made a huge difference in my life. I'm calmer, more in control of my emotions and am much more creative than I was before. I attribute my ability to manifest my amazing life here in San Miguel, Mexico, in great part to my meditation practice.

I have studied a number of different styles of meditation: Transcendental Meditation, Buddhist Insight meditation, Autogenic Conditioning, Ishaya Ascension, the Yoga techniques of Paramahansa Yogananda, Shamanic journeying, mantra, and self hypnosis. I can attest that they all work. The key is to find a style that is easy for you and that you enjoy. If you don't enjoy it, you probably won't do it.

The benefits of meditation are profound and deep, but they are subtle. If you are impatient and goal oriented like I am, this can be challenging. It's hard to quantify the results...but they are there when you look back.

Much of the time I feel as if nothing is happening and I am wasting my time. At these times it is worth remembering that almost all spiritual leaders, personal development teachers, many successful business leaders, renowned artists, writers, musicians and entertainers, most therapists and healers, and many prominent doctors highly recommend meditation. This keeps me going. They can't all be wrong.

In the past 40 years, meditation has truly entered the mainstream of modern Western culture.

Wayne Dyer, the inspirational writer and teacher, says,

"Meditation gives you an opportunity
to come to know your invisible self.
It allows you to empty yourself of
the endless hyperactivity of your mind,
and to attain calmness.

It teaches you to be peaceful,
to remove stress,
to receive answers
where confusion previously reigned."

I strongly recommend you incorporate meditation into your daily practice. It will heighten your creativity, make you calmer and more focused, and give you a peaceful outlook. It will help you know what you really want in life, write your books for you, paint your pictures, help you lose weight, learn to cook—you name it and it will help you. Well, most things. So far I haven't been able to get it to learn Spanish for me, but I'm working on it.

Returning From Your Hero's Journey

You are now returning from your *Hero's Journey*, your journey of personal evolution. This has been a journey I trust will help you transition to the next stage of your life with enthusiasm and purpose, leaving behind whatever is no longer serving you.

Life is always going to be full of changes, and when things change, you may need to stop and re-evaluate your story, and reflect on what you want to be doing with your life.

Those who have the most resources and flexibility to change are **the survivors in life's storms.**

Your desires and goals and heart's desires can change again and again and again—and that's fine. Whenever life throws you a curve ball and you experience some sort of challenge to your equilibrium, you may want to go through the steps in this book. Again. And again.

A caveat here: This book is essentially a coaching book—an alternative life-coaching handbook; it is not meant to be a spiritual guide. Having said that, it is important that you avoid identifying *with* your new story, your new roles in life. You are not your story.

Your story and your roles are there to help you along in life, your *outer purpose* as Eckhart Tolle calls it. I like to think of my new story as a loosely fitting cape that is comfortable and warm and can be changed when I no longer need it. The cape is not me.

—Instead, this book is a practical guide to growing older and helping you survive and thrive during transition times.

—It is about honoring the rebellious old hippie spirit and having a healthy skepticism for the status quo—just like you did before in the 1960s and have probably been doing all your life.

—It's about thinking for yourself, making up your own mind, and not blindly accepting the current world mindset.

Put aside the idea that the false gods of the gym, Pilates, Botox or plastic surgery are where the answers lie in aging well. They will not make you happier if you have no purpose to your life, no energizing story you are living by. These may be activities you choose to pursue but do not mistake them for a blueprint for aging happily.

I also urge you to push back against the idea, mooted in Malcom Gladwell's book, *Outliers*, that you need 10,000 hours of concentrated practice to master something new. This has been proven to be false, and it can discourage those of us in our age group (Old Hippies) from trying anything new. You **can** learn new skills quickly. It all depends on motivation and your propensity for the subject.

I'm sort of ashamed to say that I stopped going to an art class because the teacher kept telling everyone how it had taken her 40 years to get as good as she was. Well, most of us in the class didn't have 40 more years, so what was that message supposed to do for us?

I also had a Tai Chi teacher who kept repeating that it took at least 20 years to even begin to 'get' tai chi. Well, who needs that? One thing I love about Neuro-Linguistic Programming and Accelerated Learning is that they encourage everyone to try out anything they fancy. With the right attitude, focus, motivation, using all the senses, and modeling skills, anything is possible. I don't actually care if these claims are 100% true all the time—what counts to me is that they motivate.

This book has given you processes and steps to take, and searching questions to answer that will serve you through any transition and change in your life. There is no reason to get lost in the forest again, or at least not for long.

If you find yourself wandering around, stuck, afraid of getting older, you can now choose to:

Evaluate where you are and be honest about your situation.

Let go of whatever you're clinging to that is holding you back.

Retain what is working for you and that you want to keep from the past.

Enter the caves that are harboring fears you don't want to face, especially the fears around getting older.

Tame any dragons of negative emotions, limiting beliefs or bad habits that are fighting your progress and keeping you stuck.

Hold Council Meetings with your Archetypes and guides and ask for guidance. Keep asking until you get the help you need.

170

Keep asking yourself the million dollar questions in these chapters that uncover your true heart's desire. Keep asking until you get an answer that satisfies your disquiet.

Rewrite your story. Make it fit your life right now. Create the perfect recipe.

Manifest your heart's desire. Become partners with the Universe, your guides and your Higher Self to co-create a fabulous life full of passion and meaning.

You almost certainly will find you have to go through this process more than once. Personal evolution is ongoing. Change is constant. However, each time you will find it gets easier. And each time you will find you are less and less identifying with your roles and stories.

Tony Robbins says he is continually in transition and always asking himself challenging questions. "What is it I truly desire right now? What is the one thing, if I could change right now that would transform my life?"

Asking these questions keeps you fresh, inspired and passionate.

These are the steps I took and the processes I used in my own journey of personal evolution. I know that they work. They saved me when I was feeling disconnected and stuck.

The techniques in this book are the ones that really helped me transform my life into one that I really love. These are the ones that helped me find meaning and purpose when I was *with no direction home*. They helped me go from feeling like *a complete unknown* into someone I liked being with again.

Using these processes I have overcome issues around health, finances, relationship changes, losing my career, moving to another country, and being separated from everything familiar to me. They enabled me to re-design my life and awaken the Archetypes in me that helped me understand who I was.

I can still fall into the trap of fear, brought on by reading the news or listening to negative people. But I know now how to counter those fears and rebel against them. *"But I'm not giving in an inch to fear, 'cause I promised myself this year!"*

I love being able to inspire others through my coaching, therapy and writing. I enjoy being able to help others through their times of transition. I adore empowering people to face aging fearlessly, rebelliously. I want to awaken the *Old Hippie* in you and get you motoring again.

These are my passions. Now, what are yours?

Thank you for joining me in your journey. You and everyone in your life will benefit if you are active, contributing, rebelling, and living a life full of purpose. Be a role model, for the kids following you, for courageous aging.

Let's show them how it's done, with that *Old Hippie* spirit!

"Those who depart from this world without knowing who they are or what they truly desire have no freedom here or hereafter.
But those who leave here knowing who they are and what they truly desire have freedom everywhere, both in this world and in the next."

Upanishads—Sacred Song

Appendix: Archetypes

(with thanks to Caroline Myss)

Addict (Workaholic, Glutton, Conspicuous Consumer, Gambler)

The Addict hands over power to an outside substance or habit and is willing to compromise close relationships, integrity, character, or emotional, spiritual and physical well being for it. Obsession with certain behaviors. Can be funneled to good purpose such as the Workaholic who devotes himself to a good cause.

From the Shadow side the Addict represents a struggle with willpower and the absence of self-control.

Advocate (Attorney, Activist, Crusader, Defender, Environmentalist, Champion of the Underdog)

Coming to the defense of others, a lifelong devotion to championing the rights of others in the public arena. A lifelong passion to transform social concerns.

The Shadow manifests in false or negative causes or in committing to causes for personal gain. Fanatic, Terrorist.

Alchemist (Wizard, Magician, Scientist, Inventor)

A fascination with transformation whether physical, spiritual or emotional. You may identify with this archetype if you are interested in a path of spiritual development that is aligned to the mystery schools or study of the laws of the universe.

The Shadow sides of theses archetypes are found in the misuse of the power and knowledge that comes through them.

Angel (Fairy Godmother/Godfather)

If you have a strong connection to the angelic realm or embody loving or nurturing qualities, or help people anonymously, this may be one of your Archetypes.

The Shadow manifests through people who make false claims to be in touch with divine guidance for the sake of control or ego enhancement.

Artist (Musician, Author, Dramatist, Actor, Artisan, Sculptor)

This archetype embodies the passion to express a dimension of life that is just beyond the 5 senses. The Artist is animated with the energy to express it into physical forms; an emotional and psychological need to express.

The Shadow includes an eccentric nature and the madness that often accompanies genius.

Athlete (Olympian, Sportsman)

This archetype represents the expression of the strength of the human spirit in the power of the human body. A code of ethics and morality is connected to this archetype, as is dedication to transcending the limits of physical form and the development of personal will power and strength of spirit.

Avenger (Advocate, Avenging Angel)

A burning desire to defend and a passion to avenge injustices. Attorneys who work for the poor or disadvantaged, bringing war criminals to justice or pursuing modern corporations to trial are modern Avengers.

The Shadow manifests as losing a sense of proportion and becoming obsessive for revenge—eco-terrorism to bombing abortion clinics.

Beggar (Homeless Person, Indigent)

Enjoys living hand to mouth and 'trusting in the Universe to provide.' Likes being able to survive on next to nothing. Completely without material resources, the Beggar is associated with dependence on the kindness of others, living on the streets or starving for attention, love, authority, as well as material objects.

The Beggar represents a test that compels a person to confront self-empowerment beginning with physical survival. Learning about the nature of generosity, compassion and self-esteem are fundamental to this pattern.

Bully (Coward)

Shadow archetype. Consider on your life path whether you confront one experience and relationship after another that appears to have more power than you. The Coward is underneath the Bully and must learn to stand up to being bullied by his own inner fears, which is the path to empowerment through these archetypes.

Shadow of the Warrior.

Caregiver (Nurturer, Best Friend, Sister, Nurse)

Lives to give and look after others. Always lending a helping hand and listening ear. Can ignore own needs if not careful. Serene, capable, nourishing. A true Heroine.

Shadow becomes the Martyr and begins resenting those she helps.

Child (Orphan, Wounded, Magical/ Innocent, Nature, Divine, Eternal)

The Child is a universal archetype and everyone has expressions of these aspects of the Child within. The core issue of all the Child archetypes is dependency and responsibility. One of the above aspects of the Child is usually so dominant that it eclipses the energy of the others.

Child: Orphan

The pattern here is reflected in people who feel they are not a part of their family, including the tribal family or family circle. They have to develop independence early on and the absence of family influences, attitudes, and traditions forces them to construct an inner reality based on personal judgment and experience. They represent the battle with the fear of surviving alone in the world.

The Shadow manifests when they never recover and feelings of abandonment stifle their growth often causing them to seek surrogate family structures, such as therapeutic support groups or cults.

Child: Wounded

The Wounded Child holds memories of abuse, neglect, and other trauma endured in childhood and credits them with having a substantial influence on adult life.

176

Often the experiences lead to helping other Wounded Children and a path of service. The Shadow may manifest as an abiding sense of self-pity, a tendency to blame your parents for your current short comings and to resist moving forward to forgiveness.

Child: Magical /Innocent

The Magical Child represents the part of us that is both enchanted and enchanting, and sees the potential for sacred beauty in all things. It also embodies the qualities of wisdom and courage in the face of difficult circumstances. The Magical Child believes everything is possible.

The Shadow manifests in pessimism and depression and a retreat into fantasy.

Child: Divine

The Divine Child is associated with innocence, purity, and redemption qualities that suggest a special relationship with the Divine itself.

The Shadow manifests as an inability to defend itself against negative forces.

Child: Nature

A deep intimate bonding with natural forces and animals. Tender emotional qualities combined with a toughness and ability to survive. A life pattern of relating to animals in an intimate and caring way.

Child: Eternal

A determination to remain eternally young in body, mind and spirit. Age doesn't stop them from enjoying life with a healthy attitude. The Shadow manifests as an inability to grow up and embrace responsibility. No foundation for a functioning adulthood.

Clown (Court Jester, Fool, Joker)

The Clown is allowed to cross boundaries of social acceptance and is allowed into powerful circles. The Jester is the only one who can get away with making fun of the King. The Clown is able to see things as they are and to comment sharply on the hypocrisies of the day.

The Shadow manifests as cruel mockery or savage betrayal with the breaking of confidences.

Coach (Mentor, Role Model)

Assists others to see things realistically; encourages, motivates, inspires.

Companion (Friend, Sidekick, Consort, Assistant, Secretary)

Loyalty, tenacity, and unselfishness often to a personality that often has a stronger nature or role in life. Emotional support, Platonic friendship.

Damsel in Distress/Princess

The Damsel in Distress is beautiful and vulnerable and in need of rescue, specifically by a Knight, and once rescued is taken care of in lavish style. Helpless and in need of protection. Fear of going it alone. Princess is associated with having a sense of entitlement and shares the belief that she is powerless without a Knight to protect her.

Lesson is learning empowerment and learning to take care of oneself in the world.

Detective (Spy, Snoop, Profiler)

Ability to seek out knowledge and information that supports solving crimes and mysteries. Great powers of observation and intuition.

The Shadow manifests as voyeurism or falsifying information.

Dilettante (Amateur, Dabbler)

To delight in, a lover of fine arts who never rises above the level of amateur – jack of all trades, master of none. The Shadow manifests as a pretension to much deeper knowledge that you actually possess. Tendency to skim over subjects lightly.

Don Juan (Casanova, Gigolo, Seducer, Sex Addict)

Uses sex appeal for power. A need to control. Manipulative. Radiates sensuality and romantic attraction, and an attitude that all women need him more than he needs them.

The shadow side of the Lover.

Empathic (Intuitive, Psychic)

Someone who has special sensitivities to the energies of others. Can be overwhelmed by crowds, negative people. Intuitive, psychic.

Shadow is the Vampire.

Engineer (Architect, Builder, Designer, Organizer)

Practical, hands-on, devoted to making things work. Grounded, orderly, strategic. Designs solutions to everyday problems.

Exorcist (Shaman, Priest)

Ability to confront evil in the form of possession by destructive or antisocial impulses or forces that we feel are beyond our control. Notice lifelong pattern of exorcising the negative spirits or others or of social groups.

The Shadow is the charlatan, fake healer.

Father (Patriarch, Godfather, Parent)

Oversees others, courageous and protective. Guides and shields those under his care

Shadow emerges when that guidance becomes dictatorial control or abuse of authority.

The shadow is the tyrant.

Femme Fatale (Black Widow, Flirt, Seductress)

Female counterpart of Don Juan. Highly refined skills at manipulating men without investing personal emotion. Drawn to money and power for the sake of personal control and survival. Not looking for a home in the suburbs.

The shadow of the Lover.

Free Spirit (Innocent)

Optimist, playful, fun-loving. Follows her heart, not her head. Flower child, Hippie, Bohemian. Doesn't play by the rules but not rebellious.

Shadow is the Nomad, Homeless Person, Outcast.

Gambler

Risk-taker who plays the odds. Follows hunches and believes in one's intuition even in the face of doubt. Real estate, scientific research, entrepreneurs, day traders.

Shadow is addicted to risk and willing to lose everything for a hunch.

God (Adonis)

Great worldly power or great physical specimen, the ultimate in male dominance. Can be benevolent and compassionate, willing to use his powers to help others. Shadow is dictator or despot. You need to have sense of great power to claim this archetype.

Goddess

Source of all life, fertility, exaggerated sexual attributes. Fabulous woman. Can embody wisdom, guidance, physical grace, athletic prowess, and sensuality. Examine whether you associate with love and fertility, sensuality, beauty, strength, motherhood, queenship, mysticism, wisdom.

Gossip (Socialite, Schmoozer, Society Journalist)

Rumor-spreading, backbiting, and passing along information that is exaggerated and harmful. Publishes misleading information, creates damaging rumors, or hounds celebrities. Thrives on the power that is generated from passing around secret or private information. The shadow of the Networker.

Guide (Guru, Sage, Wise Woman, Spiritual Master)

Takes role of Teacher to spiritual level, teaching not only beliefs and practices of established religions, but also the principle of seeing the Divine in every aspect of life. Discern in your life a continuing pattern of devoting yourself to teaching others from your own spiritual experiences gained from self-disciplined practice and study. Passing wisdom to others.

Shadow is the Guru who is interested in power, money and ego.

Healer (Intuitive, Caregiver, Therapist, Nurse, Analyst, Doctor)

Passion to serve others in the form of repairing the body, mind and spirit.

Wounded Healer (Shaman)

Initiated into the art of healing through some form of personal hardship - injury or illness or loss of all one's earthly possessions. If you pass the test of initiation and healing, a path of service seems to be divinely provided shortly after the initiation is complete.

Shadow manifests in claiming to be able to heal any and every illness a person has.

Hedonist (Bon Vivant, Chef, Gourmet)

An appetite for pleasurable aspects of life from good food and wine to sexuality and sensuality. Indulging the self is central to this archetype.

Shadow manifests as pursuing pleasure without regard for health or other people. Addiction or overweight is symptom of Shadow.

Hero/Heroine (Fireman, Rescuer, Knight)

Capable of great feats of strength or skill. An icon of power. Usually goes on journey where he or she defeats enemies – a journey of initiation to awaken an inner knowledge or spiritual power. Confronts survival fears in the form of demons or dragons and returns to the tribe with something of great value for all.

Innocent

Similar to the Virgin – pure, transparent, lacking underhanded intentions. Free Spirit, naïve,optimist.

Shadow is the Cynic, disillusioned with betrayal.

Intellectual (Professor, Scholar, Academic)

Rational, well read, scholarly, seeks knowledge and wisdom. Well informed. Well educated. Approaches life from a mental platform.

Loves knowledge for the sake of it.

The shadow can become more interested in cleverness than wisdom.

Judge (Critic, Mediator, Arbitrator)

Vision to manage fair distribution of power. Involved in interventions between people. Leads life of high standards related to justice and wisdom.

Shadow manifest destructive criticism, judgment without compassion or hidden agendas. Misuse of authority.

King (Emperor, Ruler, Chief)

Represents the height of male power and authority. Can be both benevolent and cruel. Attitude of entitlement and resistance to criticism, questioning, and challenges in decisions about controlling his kingdom. Need to rule and exert control over a kingdom.

Shadow is the Tyrant, Dictator.

Knight (Knight, Hero, Rescuer, Warrior)

Associated with chivalry, courtly romance and protection of the Princess and going to battle for honorable causes.

Shadow has the power without honor and chivalry – Mercenary, Gun for Hire.

Liberator

Helps to liberate us from the tyranny of negative thought patterns and beliefs, spiritual sluggishness, poor nutrition, destructive relationships. Frees us from old entrenched beliefs and attitudes. Shadow manifests as one who imposes his own tyranny - corporate, political, religious, and spiritual leaders.

183

Lost Soul

Sensitive, tortured, brooding, poetic, wanderer, outcast, creative, loner. Attractive to opposite sex.
Shadow of the Seeker, Mystic.

Lover

Loves passionately whether in romance, art, music, animals, gardening, poetry. A sense of unbridled and exaggerated affection and appreciation of someone or something in your life that influences the organization of your life and environment.

The Shadow manifests as an exaggerated, obsessive passion that has a destructive effect on one's physical or mental health – Addict, Stalker, Don Juan, Seductress, Black Widow.

Magician (Shaman, Witch, Warlock, Alchemist)

Fascinated with transformation whether external or internal. The Magician is also known as the Visionary, Catalyst, Shaman, Healer, Medicine Man.

Shadow is the charlatan, fake, pretend healer – after fame, money, power.

Martyr

Suffering for the redemption others whether that redemption takes a spiritual or political form. Dying for a cause.

Shadow manifests as manipulating others by serving and suffering for them - Victim

Maverick

Lives just on the outskirts of society but not an outcast. Follows his own rules. Male version of the Free spirit. Frequently a loner, nomad, wanderer.

Shadow is the Outcast, Rogue. No accepted by society because he goes to far in following his own path.

Mediator (Ambassador, Diplomat, Go-Between)

Smoothes relations between antagonistic groups or individuals. Has patience and skill and an ability to read people and situations with great acuity. Respects both sides of an argument or cause. Lifelong commitment to resolving disputes and bringing people together.

Mentor (Master, Counselor, Tutor, Coach, Guru, Guide)

More than a Teacher, Mentors pass on wisdom and refine their student's character. Usually an individual student is taken under the Mentor's wing and guided in many aspects of life.

Shadow Mentor shows an inability to allow the student to develop to the role of master, jealousy.

Messiah (Redeemer, Savior)

Embodiment of divine power and having a mission from heaven to save humanity. Shadow becomes obsessed with his spiritual purpose, convinced that God needs him to do something.

Midas

Midas has entrepreneurial or creative ability. Ability to generate wealth seemingly easily.

Shadow is Miser - creates wealth and hoards it. A need to control the forces around you for fear of losing your wealth.

Missionary

Possesses absolute certainty about beliefs. No doubts or skepticism. Not looking for answers – has found them. Keen to share beliefs with any and everyone.

Shadow is fanatic who cares more about beliefs than compassion.

Monk/Nun (Renunciate)

Spiritual intensity, devotion, dedication, persistence, wisdom. Devoted to the spiritual path or to any great achievement that requires intense focus. Single minded dedication, relinquishing material desires and ambitions to pursue spiritual practice; can withdraw from the world to pursue the spiritual path or to pursue a solitary life.

Shadow is overly pious or privileged. Overly reclusive, not involved in the world – Hermit.

Mother (Caregiver, Nurturer, Earth Mother)

Life-giver, source of nurturing and nourishment, unconditional fountain of love, patience, devotion, caring and unselfish. Keeper and protector of life. Power of compassion and endless capacity to forgive her children. The Devouring, Abusive, Abandoning Mother represent the Shadow. Also protecting the environment, gardening or supporting any life form.

Mystic (Yogi)

A fascination for the otherworldly, the spiritual, the arcane, the magical, the occult. Can claim direct communication with the divine. Initiate in religious mysteries.

Shadow is egotistical concern for one's own spiritual progress to the exclusion of others or self importance at having achieved higher states of consciousness. Drug Addict.

Networker (Communicator, Messenger, Journalist)

Expands sphere of influence by forging alliances and making connections. Skill to bring information and inspiration to disparate groups of people. Brings people together.

Shadow is the Gossip, Society Journalist, Paparazzi.

Pioneer (Explorer, Settler, Innovator, Entrepreneur)

Called to discover and explore new lands, whether internal or external. Passion to explore, initiate, innovate. A need to step onto fresh and undiscovered territory in at least one realm.

Shadow manifests as compulsive need to abandon one's past and move on to new conquests – Vagabond, Gypsy, Traveler, Homeless Person, Beggar.

Pirate (Swashbuckler)

Pirates were thieves of the open seas pursuing rich treasures and burying them in caves, creating legends around buried treasure within the caves of our inner being. Symbolize freedom and ability to strike back at wealthy and aristocratic. Steal everything from intellectual property to information via the Internet.

Shadow of the Adventurer, Pioneer, Explorer., Swashbuckler.

Poet

Combines lyricism with sharp insight finding the essence of beauty and truth in everything. You need to be driven by the need and ability to discover beauty in the people and things around you and express it in a way that helps others see that beauty too.

Shadow is the Madman, Addict, Beggar, Homeless Person. Can sacrifice everything for his art.

Priest /Priestess

Official capacity to make spiritual vows, ordination and perform rituals of initiation – commitments made to divine authority. Power to covey to the public the power of sacred teachings, rituals, wisdom and ethics of each spiritual tradition.

Shadow is the Hypocrite, TeleEvangelist, who doesn't walk his talk.

Prince

Royal but not the ruler in charge. Shows leadership, responsibility to the kingdom. Humanitarian. Compassionate and humble.

Shadow can have feelings of entitlement as an heir apparent who uses his position to advance himself. Spoiled or Lazy Prince thinks the world owes him a living without responsibility or needing to work for a living.

Princess

Female royal. Similar to Prince. Princess can be compassionate, caring for the poor, the destitute. Beautiful, generous spirited.

Shadow is Lazy Princess, entitled, doesn't want to support herself. Dependent on the King for support. Daddy's Little Princess.

Prostitute

Shadow archetype. Sale or negotiation of one's integrity or spirit due to fears of physical and financial survival. Seduction and control. Selling of talents or selling out. Frequently related to one's job or relationship.

Shadow of the Survivor.

Queen

Power and authority in a woman. Court can be company or home. Shadow associated with arrogance and a defensive posture showing need to protect one's personal and emotional power. Can be lonely, cold, and icy. Queens do not like challenges to their control, authority and leadership. Drama Queen.

Rebel (Non-conformist, Free Spirit, Misfit, Iconoclast, Revolutionary)

Powerful aid in helping break away from old tribal patterns or spiritual systems that do not serve your inner needs. May reject legitimate authority simply for the sake of it.

Shadow is Rogue, Outcast.

Rescuer (Fireman, Knight, Hero)

Assists when needed and then withdraws. Provides an infusion of strength and support to help others survive a difficult situation, crisis or process. Shadow shows itself in relationships where the Rescuer hopes to forge an intimate, romantic bond with the one being rescued.

Shadow is Vigilante.

Ruler (Godfather, King)

Creates a prosperous family or community, tribe or nation. Also known as boss, leader, manager. Shadow is Tyrant, dictator, corrupt politician.

Saboteur

Shadow archetype. Embodies fears and issues related to self esteem that cause one to make choices that block one's own empowerment. Self destructive.

Sage

Wise person, knowledgeable, with perspective. Philosopher, Elder.

Samaritan (Rescuer)

Closely related to Martyr. Makes sacrifices for those they are least inclined to serve. Shadow shows as one who helps one to the detriment of another with a kind of self importance.

Seductress (Black Widow)

Shadow archetype. Enchantress, Flirt, uses sexual attraction for power. Used to getting her way, manipulative. Strong survival instincts. Interested in men for what they can give her.

Shadow of the Lover.

Seeker (Wanderer, Nomad, Explorer)

One who searches for God or enlightenment. In search of wisdom and truth wherever it is to be found. Always interested in new paths, religions, teachers, wisdom literature.

The Shadow is the lost soul, on an aimless journey without direction, disconnected from goals and others.

Servant (Caretaker)

Available to others for the benefit and enhancement of their lives. The shadow is The Indentured Servant who sees himself bound by conditions of service that he cannot get out of, for example someone in an unhappy relationship who is waiting to get enough money to leave, to buy their freedom. Shadow also the Victim.

Shaman (Medicine Man, Witch, Sorcerer)

Special abilities – magic, transformation, healing, psychic powers. Uses magic to cure illness, foretell the future, control the forces of nature. Fascination with the occult and with spiritual forces. Connection with nature, herbs, animals, spiritual guides.

Shadow is the fake; the pretender interested in followers and money and power.

Shaper-shifter (Actor)

Can navigate through different levels of consciousness, both dream and waking states. Can reinvent to appeal to latest popular trends. Can change appearance and personality as well as convictions and beliefs to fit in. Good archetype for actors, entertainers or ambassadors.

Shadow side is when you change so often nobody knows who you really are. Lacking conviction.

Slave (Puppet)

Shadow archetype. A complete absence of the power of choice and self authority. Act of releasing will to higher authority can be very spiritual but can also be seen in corporations and in the military or church. Can be manipulated by others.

Shadow of the Servant.

Storyteller (Entertainer, Novelist)

Relays wisdom, foolishness, mistakes, successes, fact and fiction and tales of love. Essential to their way of communicating and perceiving the world. Writers, Teachers, can be Storytellers. Shadow is liar and exaggerator. Society Journalist.

Student (Disciple, Devotee, Follower)

A pattern of constant learning, an openness to absorbing new information as an essential part of one's well-being. Loves learning anything new. Loves continuous education.

Shadow can show as Eternal Student who never embarks on the sea of life in earnest, but manages to find new reasons to continue being schooled without ever putting that knowledge to the test.

Uses the excuse that they are not ready or have not learned enough to advance their dreams to reality. Suggests an absence of mastery of any one subject but rather continual pursuit of intellectual development.

Teacher

Passion to communicate knowledge, experience, skill and wisdom. Loves a soapbox, classroom, audience.

Shadow more concerned with recognition than with imparting knowledge. Bullies or manipulates students.

Thief (Pirate)

Shadow archetype. Plagiarism or stealing of any kind including ideas and affection. Taking what is not yours because you lack the ability to provide for yourself whether materially or in the emotional and intellectual arenas.

Shadow of the Swashbuckler.

Trickster

Jokester, Clown, Court Jester. Mischievous, calls out hypocrisy, likes to play jokes and tricks.

Vampire (Black Widow)

Shadow archetype. Drains the energy of others for his or her own psychic survival. Needy emotionally. A need for approval, a need to be taken care of and a fear of being abandoned. Co-dependent relationships. Seen in chronic complaining, over dependency, or holding onto relationships long after their sell by date. Chronic power struggles.

Shadow of the Lover.

Victim

Shadow archetype. The poor-me syndrome, blaming others for problems or issues. Or victimizing others. Looks for sympathy or pity.

Shadow of the Child.

Virgin

Associated with purity, innocence. A trusting outlook on the world. Shadow manifests in prudish disgust with or fear of sex.

Visionary (Mystic, Prophet, Shaman)

Has large vision and can imagine possibilities beyond the normal. Messages associated with divine guidance that can benefit all of society. Can see what is in the future.

Shadow is charlatan psychic, or power mad leader such as Mao or Stalin.

Warrior (Amazon, Soldier)

Physical strength and the ability to protect, defend and fight for rights. Similar to Knight, but Knight is romantic. Warrior is invincible and loyal. The willingness to face challenges and fight battles.

Women warriors, Amazons, are fierce to defend their families and are loyal and brave.

Shadow is Mercenary, Gun for Hire.

Witch (Empath, Intuitive, Herbalist)

Female who practices magic, the magic arts, herbalism, animals, connection to nature. Fascinated with nature and spirits. A healer.

Shadow is Black Witch who uses powers to hurt others.

About Margaret Nash

Margaret Nash was born in the Deep South, a preacher's kid, and grew up in Alabama in the turbulent and trail-blazing 1960s. After college in Atlanta she visited Scotland where she met and married an Englishman, and stayed for three decades.

She currently lives in San Miguel de Allende, an alternative, artistic haven in the central mountains of Mexico, with her second husband, who is Mexican. She spends her time as a life-coach, hypnotherapist, self-help writer, and workshop leader, in sun-drenched San Miguel.

Margaret's blog—*the old hippie at heart*—and her books, *Rebellious Aging,* and *How To Get Along With Everybody, All the Time,* deal with the themes of aging well, surviving transitions, and finding your niche in life in your 50s, 60s, and beyond. Her tribe is the aging-rebel-old-hippie who is facing major life changes and wants to age in the coolest way possible—rebelliously.

Margaret qualified with some major names in the NLP (Neuro-Linguistic Programming) world, and is a Master Practitioner/Coach in NLP, Hypnosis, and Time-line Therapy.

Margaret is a *certified* rebellious, adventurous, seeker, animal loving weirdo.

She is definitely an old hippie at heart.

www.margaretnashcoach.com
www.oldhippieatheart.com

Made in the USA
Middletown, DE
02 May 2018